GROWING
HERBS

GROWING
HERBS

Deni Bown

DORLING KINDERSLEY
London • New York • Stuttgart

A DORLING KINDERSLEY BOOK

Project Editor Martha Swift
Art Editor Alison Verity
Managing Editor
Krystyna Mayer
Managing Art Editor
Derek Coombes
US Editor Mary Sutherland
US Consultant Ray Rogers
DTP Designer Cressida Joyce
Production Controller
Ruth Charlton

First American Edition, 1995
2 4 6 8 10 9 7 5 3 1

Published in the United States by
Dorling Kindersley Publishing, Inc.,
95 Madison Avenue,
New York 10016

Copyright © 1995
Dorling Kindersley Limited,
London
Text copyright © 1995 Deni Bown

Published in Great Britain by
Dorling Kindersley Limited.
Distributed by Houghton Mifflin
Company, Boston.

Bown, Deni.
Growing herbs/by Deni Bown. -- 1st American ed.
  p. cm.
Includes index.
1. Herb gardening. 2. Herbs. I. Title.
SB351. H5B646 1995
635' .7- - dc20
                    95-19034
                       CIP
ISBN 0-7894-0191-6

Color reproduced by
Euroscan, Nottingham,
Great Britain

Printed and bound in Singapore
by Tien Wah Press

CONTENTS

INTRODUCTION

Herb growing has a special appeal, being both practical and enjoyable. Although herbs are valued primarily for their culinary, healing, and cosmetic uses, they also have the charm of wild flowers and evocative scents, which give the herb garden its uniquely restful atmosphere.

Some of the earliest herb gardens were planted 2,000 years ago in Egypt. They consisted of geometric beds, and were enclosed by walls to give protection against animals, and make the best use of shelter and water. Herbs were especially important in ritual; for example, chamomile was an ingredient of the embalming oil used to mummify pharaohs. Christian monasteries began in northern Egypt in AD 305. Monastic rule dictated that they grew culinary and medicinal herbs and aromatics for incense, as well as vegetables, fruit, and dye plants. The 9th-century plan for St. Gall in Switzerland shows an enclosed garden and rectangular beds, designed along Egyptian lines. It was copied throughout Europe. The list of "herbs both beautiful and health-giving" included savory, rose, sage, fennel, tansy, peppermint, rosemary, parsley, dill, and poppies. All are described in this book. Herb growing today is more flexible in design and purpose, from entire herb gardens to containers. Whatever the scale, it is satisfying to create a pleasing effect. To help you choose suitable plants, this book describes 60 different herbs and more than 55 variations, all of which are easy to grow, even by beginners.

A WALLED TOWN GARDEN
Herb gardens in medieval times followed monastic designs, with small, rectangular beds enclosed by walls or fences.

HOW THIS BOOK WORKS

This book contains 60 of the most common and easily grown herbs, which are arranged alphabetically by their scientific names. The sample page below shows a typical entry.

SAMPLE PAGE

Herb number corresponds to number on pull-out chart (see below)

Scientific name

Common name

Scientific family name

Description of plant's history and uses

Planting tips and associations

Related species, forms, varieties, hybrids, or cultivars

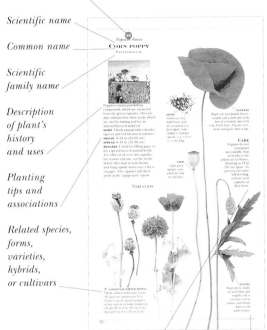

Basic care information

Annotations describing each part of plant in detail

PULL-OUT CHART

The chart lists herbs from 1 to 60. The numbers correspond with the numbers for the herb entries in the book *(see sample page above)*.

When chart is pulled down, purple strip indicates herb for which cultivation details are displayed below

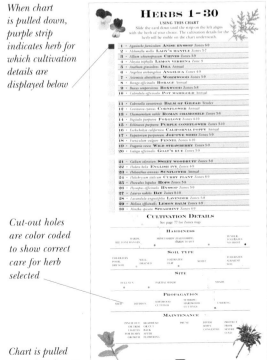

Cut-out holes are color coded to show correct care for herb selected

Chart is pulled down from bottom

DEFINING AN HERB

There are two distinct meanings of the word "herb." One is botanical, meaning a nonwoody plant, from which we get the term "herbaceous"; and the other refers to any plant that has therapeutic properties. Although we tend to think of herbs as small, aromatic plants, such as parsley and thyme, they include a very wide range of plants, from annuals, biennials, and herbaceous perennials to trees, shrubs, climbers, and primitive plants, such as ferns and mosses. Some herbs are not especially aromatic, and others may even smell unpleasant – for example, a boxwood hedge after clipping.

SCIENTIFIC TERMS

Just as we devise a family tree to explain our origins, plants are classified according to their relationships, which are based mainly on the structure of floral parts. The classification gives each plant a scientific name in Latin, which is accepted worldwide. This eliminates misunderstandings that would occur if common names in different languages were used.
A plant's scientific name has two main parts, rather like a last name and a first name, for example, *Symphytum officinale*.

The basic relationships are:

FAMILY
A group of related genera. Example: Boraginaceae.

GENUS (plural GENERA)
A group of related species, indicated by the first part of the Latin name. Example: *Symphytum*.

SPECIES
Individuals that are alike and naturally breed with each other, denoted by the second part of the Latin name. Examples: *Symphytum asperum* (Prickly comfrey) or *Symphytum officinale* (Common comfrey).

HYBRID
A cross between two species, which sometimes happens in the wild, but more usually occurs accidentally or artificially in cultivation. It is given a different name from either parent, with an "x" to show hybrid status. Example: *Symphytum* x *uplandicum* (Russian comfrey). Parents are sometimes given in brackets after the hybrid name. Example: *Symphytum* x *uplandicum (S. asperum* x *S. officinale)*.

VARIETY, SUBSPECIES, AND FORM
(often given as var., subsp., or f.)
Subdivisions within a species or natural hybrid that differ consistently in small but distinct ways from the type. These natural variants are often rare in the wild, but common in cultivation, offering attractive differences in habit, color, and so on. Example: *Symphytum officinale* var. *ochroleucum* (White-flowered comfrey).

CULTIVAR
A variant produced and maintained by cultivation, which has desirable characteristics of habit, color, and flavor.
Example: *Symphytum* x *uplandicum* 'Variegatum' (Variegated Russian comfrey).

TYPES OF HERB GARDEN

The only definition of an herb garden is that it is where herbs are grown. It might be based on a formal design, such as a knot garden or a simple border. At its smallest, it can consist of a window box, a cartwheel, or a collection of herbs in pots.

THE TRADITIONAL HERB GARDEN IS usually divided by paths into orderly, geometric beds. It is usually enclosed, with a central feature and a sheltered place to sit, making a peaceful retreat. The beds may be raised, to give better drainage, and edged by tiles or timber to hold the soil. Tudor gardens were often framed by low

AN OPEN KNOT GARDEN
The pattern in this walled garden is defined by paths made from old bricks, which soften the geometric lines and create a walkway through the herbs.

hedges of aromatic herbs, such as lavender, on which washing was spread out to dry. Designs based on dwarf hedges are known as knot gardens; the beds are either planted with herbs or filled with gravel. Few original knot gardens remain, but re-creations have been made in some large gardens and at many herb nurseries. Larger, more elaborate knot gardens are known as *parterres*.

INFORMAL DESIGNS

An informal herb garden, planted in the relaxed style of a herbaceous border or cottage garden, can create effects based on complementary habits and colors. It may include herbs that might be out of place in a formal garden, such as large shrubs, invasive mints, giant angelica, or small

creeping thymes. A compromise between formal and informal is often successful. The Queen's Garden at Kew in west London has a formal structure of terraces above a sunken garden, which consists of two large, rectangular beds. Plantings are all informal, displaying herbs of the 17th century.

HERBS WITH OTHER GARDEN PLANTS

In many gardens, herbs have to take their places beside other kinds of plant. Many herbs are ornamental border plants in their own right – bee balm, rue, and purple sage are examples. Various thymes are often sold as rock-garden plants, and creeping herbs of all kinds can be planted in gravel or paving to form a fragrant carpet that stands the occasional

STRAWBERRY POT
This is an attractive and practical way of growing seven or more herbs vertically. A pot made from terracotta is much more stable than a plastic one.

footstep. Small, neat herbs are suitable for edging; wall germander is good beside paths, and culinary herbs, such as curly parsley and chives, are attractive around a vegetable plot. Scented geraniums and colorful annuals, such as poppies and cornflowers, are useful for filling gaps in a

HANGING BASKET
This is a good way of growing small and compact herbs, although they must be resilient to withstand wind damage.

Growing herbs in containers has several advantages – the plants are easy to replace so at least one can always be at its best, and all but the largest containers are movable. The only disadvantages are that the plants require regular watering and feeding, and need repotting or replacing every spring. Containers are especially useful for certain herbs. They are ideal for confining invasive mints, and for leafy culinary herbs, such as basil. Containerized specimen shrubs of boxwood or bay, clipped into topiary shapes, create instant focal points. If grown in pots, slightly hardy herbs, such as lemon verbena and myrtle, can be conveniently brought under cover in cold weather. A window box, hanging basket, or strawberry

HERB TOWER
Chives, thyme, marjoram, mint, purple sage, and parsley have been planted in this container, which was constructed from moss and chicken wire.

FORMAL ARRANGEMENT
A neat way of growing a variety of herbs in a formal manner is to plant them in a small, circular, brick-edged bed.

border. Lavender and rosemary are most enjoyed near a seat or entrance, where a fragrant sprig can be picked as you pass.

HERBS IN CONTAINERS

Many herbs grow well in containers. In small gardens or on balconies, the entire herb garden may consist of containers, imaginatively positioned on walls, steps, shelves, and windowsills. Almost any container is suitable, provided that it has drainage holes to prevent waterlogging.

pot (a large pot with planting pockets), planted with a collection of herbs, makes an interesting feature that takes up little space. When planting a mixture of herbs in the same container, try to avoid very tall herbs and include small-growing types.

CREATING AN HERB GARDEN

*Whatever the style of herb garden, much satisfaction
comes from planting the herbs in attractive combinations.
There is a wide choice of herbs to grow, especially
of variants that have different habits and colors,
and often make better garden plants than the wild species.*

MOST HERBS PREFER AN OPEN, SUNNY, well-drained site, and neutral to alkaline soil. Plan the layout of the garden carefully, drawing it to scale if necessary. Remember that small beds give easier access for maintenance and harvesting than large ones, and provide stepping stones in large beds to prevent trampling and compaction. Transfer the design to the ground, using pegs and string, before making beds and paths. Prepare the soil by removing weeds

GOLDEN BORDER
This border combines fennel (*Foeniculum vulgare*) and tansy (*Tanacetum vulgare*) with golden hops (*Humulus lupulus* 'Aureus') and golden marjoram (*Origanum vulgare* 'Aureum'). The colors are complementary, and there are strong contrasts in shape and texture.

and then by forking in manure or compost. Drainage can be improved by adding gravel, and by raising or sloping the beds.

CHOOSING HERBS

Herb nurseries offer the widest range of herbs, but garden centers are good for popular herbs and for variants that may suit certain situations. Upright, prostrate, and compact variants give contrasts in height and shape; variants with bronze, variegated, or golden foliage inspire exciting color combinations. Before buying, check the requirements of each herb.

CREEPING THYMES
These soften the wooden edging and are good for gaps in the paving.

HEN-AND-CHICKENS
Like creeping thymes, these plants enjoy dry, sunny conditions at the edges of paths.

HERBS IN THE BORDER
This plan makes use of contrasting heights, habits, and colors. Each herb is allowed sufficient space for its height and spread, giving good ground cover without overcrowding. The raised bed has a wooden edging to retain the soil, and is accessed by paths.

PLANTING

Like any plant, herbs will do best in the right conditions. For example, Mediterranean herbs enjoy dry, sunny positions, woodland herbs prefer dappled shade, and variegated and golden variants retain their colors best in positions shaded at midday. Take note of the eventual height and spread, since a common mistake is to plant too close together. Container-grown herbs can be planted at any time, but will establish quickest in spring. If kept under cover, they should be acclimatized ("hardened off") before planting. First set out the plants in their pots to check arrangement and planting distances. Water them thoroughly before planting, as dry root balls are difficult to wet once below ground, and again after planting to provide even moisture for root growth. Pinch out any growing tips to encourage new sideshoots and a bushy habit.

MIXED COLORS
The small, colorful flowers of heartsease (*Viola tricolor*) are given greater impact by a background of purple sage (*Salvia officinalis* 'Purpurascens').

MAINTENANCE

Most herbs are naturally vigorous and will require little attention when established. Maintenance consists largely of cutting back plants in winter to remove dead stems, and in spring and summer to encourage strong new growth. Deadheading prolongs flowering and prevents excessive self-seeding. Clump-forming perennials need dividing every few years to maintain vigor. Invasive herbs, such as mints and tansy, may need annual division and removal of excessive new growth. Mulch the herb garden in spring with a layer of well-rotted manure or compost. If pests or diseases become a problem, improve ventilation and feeding, but use only organic sprays on herbs that will be harvested. In cold areas protect vulnerable herbs with a layer of straw or leaves around the base and some loosely woven row cover over the foliage.

VARIEGATED RUE
This variegated plant, with some completely white leaves, stands out well against simpler, darker foliage. It should be pruned hard in spring to retain its variegation.

GOLD-VARIEGATED SAGE
An excellent plant for the fronts of borders, since it retains its habit and color well. It will also add color to pots of plain green culinary herbs.

Agastache foeniculum
ANISE HYSSOP
LABIATAE

This anise-scented herb is a rich source of nectar, and attracts bees throughout its flowering period.
HABIT Hardy perennial, which forms upright clumps of stems with pointed leaves. Bold spikes of light purple flowers in summer. Dies down completely in winter.
HEIGHT 2–3 ft (60 cm–1 m).
SPREAD 18 in (45 cm).
REMARKS Attractive with gray-leaved herbs, such as artemisias, lavender cotton (*Santolina chamaecyparissus*), and curry plant (*Helichrysum italicum*). It will tolerate poor, dry soils. If you grow your own plants from seed, the odd one may have white flowers.

FLOWERS
Light purple, often with purple-tinged bracts, from midsummer to early autumn.

VARIATION

A. rugosa
(**KOREAN MINT**)
This Chinese medicinal herb enjoys damper conditions than *A. foeniculum.* Leaves have a mintlike aroma. Tiny purple flowers appear in late summer. Height 3–4 ft (1–1.2 m). Spread 2 ft (60 cm).

CARE
Cut down dead stems in winter. Mulch with well-rotted manure or compost in spring. Plants may be short-lived, so propagate every second or third year.

LEAVES
Anise-scented, pointed, and oval, with toothed margins and pale undersides. Leaves become smaller higher up the stem.

STEM
Four-angled, more or less smooth, and branched toward the top.

FLOWERS
*Tiny, lime green, and
star-shaped, produced
in delicately branched
clusters in summer.*

2

Alchemilla mollis
LADY'S MANTLE
ROSACEAE

Various kinds of Lady's mantle
are used medicinally for female
complaints. They have beautifully
shaped leaves that hold water
drops, creating an ornamental
feature after rain or dew.

HABIT Hardy perennial with broad,
rounded leaves and branched heads
of tiny green flowers in summer.

HEIGHT 12–18 in (30–45 cm).

SPREAD 12–15 in (30–38 cm).

REMARKS Complements most
garden plants and other herbs,
especially roses and lavenders.
A versatile plant that will grow in a
wide range of situations. Allow it to
self-seed in gravel or paving cracks,
or try it as groundcover. It may self-
sow excessively in some gardens.

CARE
Cut back to within 1 in
(2.5 cm) of ground level
after flowering to give fresh
new leaves that will remain
attractive until winter.

STEM
*Hairy, ridged, and
green, branching as
flowers develop, and
tending to flop as
flowering begins.*

LEAVES
*Soft, downy, and almost
circular, with seven to eleven
rounded lobes, neatly indented
along the margin. The leaves
are mostly long-stalked, with
smaller, short-stalked ones
higher up the stem.*

VARIATION

**A. alpina
(ALPINE LADY'S
MANTLE)**
Mound-forming. Ideal
for rock gardens, troughs,
and crevices. Height and
spread 4–8 in (10–20 cm).

13

Allium schoenoprasum
CHIVES
LILIACEAE

An oniony-tasting herb which
is indispensable for flavoring
and garnishing, and is best used
fresh from the garden.

HABIT Clump-forming, hardy
perennial with hollow, cylindrical
leaves, and rounded clusters of
pale purple flowers in summer.
HEIGHT 4–24 in (10–60 cm).
SPREAD 12 in (30 cm).
REMARKS An excellent herb for
edging borders. Effective with
origanums (*Origanum* species) in
sunny positions, or with bee balm
(*Monarda didyma*) and sweet cicely
(*Myrrhis odorata*) in rich, moist soil.
Planting chives around roses may
help prevent blackspot.

LEAVES
*Cylindrical and hollow,
tapering to a point,
and up to 10 in
(25 cm) in length.*

CARE
New shoots appear
very early in mild
areas, so mulch with
well-rotted manure or
compost in late winter.
Cut down to the
ground after flowering
to produce a fresh
crop of leaves. Remove
dead stems in winter.

FLOWERS
*Pale purple, bell-
shaped in rounded
clusters about
1 in (2.5 cm)
across, in summer.*

VARIATIONS

A. s. 'FORESCATE'
Larger than ordinary
chives, with pink flowers.
Height 18 in (45 cm).
Spread 12–18 in
(30–45 cm).

**A. tricoccum
(RAMPS)**
This has garlic-
flavored bulbs and
foliage and white flowers
in spring. It likes damp,
shady conditions. Height
and spread 12 in (30 cm).

FLOWERS
Tiny, pale lilac to white, appearing in loose spikes during summer.

LEAVES
Slender and light green, up to 4 in (10 cm) long, and short-stalked. Leaves are arranged in threes, and have a rough texture, and a strong lemon scent.

CARE
Cut back main stems to 12 in (30 cm), and sideshoots to within two or three buds of the old wood in spring. Remove dead wood in early summer. Repot container-grown plants in spring, or top-dress with fresh compost. Remove dead flower heads and trim untidy shoots after flowering.

STEM
Slender, brown, and woody.

Aloysia triphylla
LEMON VERBENA
VERBENACEAE

This South American shrub has a delicious lemon scent. The dried leaves retain their fragrance well, and are useful ingredients of potpourris and tisanes.
HABIT Frost-hardy, deciduous shrub, with tiny flowers in summer.
HEIGHT 3–10 ft (1–3 m).
SPREAD 3–10 ft (1–3 m).
REMARKS Needs a warm, sheltered position in cold areas. Frosted plants may be slow to recover, but usually sprout from the base by early summer. Grow pots of lemon verbena near seats and entrances, or plant in containers with black basil (*Ocimum basilicum* 'Dark Opal').

15

Anethum graveolens
DILL
UMBELLIFERAE

SEEDS
*Aromatic, and a dark
brown color. Flattened
and oval in shape,
they measure
0.2 in (5 mm).*

An important medicinal herb
in the Middle East since bibilical
times, dill is now best known as an
ingredient of Scandinavian dishes,
especially with fish. It is an excellent
remedy for digestive disorders.
HABIT Hardy annual or biennial
with foliage that is divided into
threadlike segments.
HEIGHT 2–3 ft (60 cm–1 m).
SPREAD 2–12 in (5–30 cm).
REMARKS Provides a pretty foil for
orange pot marigolds (*Calendula
officinalis*) and yellow evening
primroses (*Oenothera biennis*). The
flowers attract beneficial insects,
such as lacewings and hoverflies,
whose larvae prey on aphids.

LEAVES
*Gray-green in color,
with a waxy bloom.
They have a strong
parsley-caraway aroma.*

CARE
May be grown for foliage or seeds
from sowings made in spring or
summer. For a regular supply of fresh
leaves, sow every 3–4 weeks from early
spring to midsummer. Does not
transplant well, so sow *in situ*, thinning
to 8 in (20 cm) apart. Tends to "bolt"
(flower prematurely) in poor soil,
or if the seedlings are overcrowded.

FLOWERS
*Tiny and yellow,
produced in flat-
topped clusters.*

STEM
*Upright and
hollow, with a
blue-green color.*

LEAVES
Aromatic and long-stalked. They are deeply divided and have irregularly toothed margins.

SEEDS
Oval-oblong and flattened, with winged ridges. Sow angelica seeds when fresh, since they do not store well.

Angelica archangelica
ANGELICA
UMBELLIFERAE

Angelica was known as *herba angelica* (angelic herb) in medieval times, because it was believed to cure all ills. An important medicinal herb, it can be used to flavor liqueurs or candied for cake decoration.

HABIT Giant, hardy biennial, or short-lived perennial. Tiny greenish white flowers appear in flat-topped clusters in late spring and summer.

HEIGHT 3–8 ft (1–2.5 m).

SPREAD 18 in–4 ft (45 cm–1.2 m).

REMARKS An architectural plant for the back of the border. It overpowers most smaller herbs, but is a match for Joe-Pye weed (*Eupatorium purpureum*). It may self-sow prolifically.

CARE
Make sure that seedlings have sufficient room to develop, since they can smother smaller plants. Remove dead flower heads to prevent excessive self-seeding, or cut and dry seed heads for ornament while the seeds are still green and unripe. Mulch second-year plants with well-rotted manure or compost in spring to produce very large plants.

STEM
Green, hollow, and ridged, this can be up to 2.4 in (6 cm) in diameter.

17

Artemisia absinthium

WORMWOOD

COMPOSITAE

Artemisias include some of the bitterest herbs known; hence the expression "as bitter as wormwood," dating to biblical times. Wormwood was used as a household remedy to stimulate the digestive system.
HABIT Hardy, shrubby perennial, with gray-green foliage and tiny, dull yellow flowers in summer.
HEIGHT 3 ft (1 m).
SPREAD 10–36 in (25 cm–1 m).
REMARKS An excellent, easily grown plant for poor, dry soils. Effective in a white border, and also with dark-leaved plants, such as bronze fennel (*Foeniculum vulgare* 'Purpureum'). May also be planted as an informal hedge.

A. caucasica
(**SYN.** *A. lanata*)
Tufted, mat-forming, hardy shrublet with finely cut, fernlike foliage, silver-green in color, and aromatic. Loose clusters of tiny, round yellow flowers in summer. Good for edging. Height and spread 6–12 in (15–30 cm).

A. arborescens
Half-hardy, aromatic, shrubby perennial with a rounded habit. It is recommended for alkaline soils. Height and spread 3.5 ft (1.1 m).

LEAVES
Aromatic, silver-green, silky, and finely divided into narrow segments.

FLOWERS
Tiny, nodding yellow flowers in slender clusters, which give a graceful effect.

A. a. 'LAMBROOK SILVER'
This has luxuriant, silver-gray foliage. It makes a good background for red-purple herbs. Height 18–32 in (45–80 cm). Spread 20 in (50 cm).

STEM
Upright and grooved to angled, light green with a silky hairy texture, becoming woody at the base.

VARIATIONS

A. lactiflora
(WHITE MUGWORT)
Vigorous, hardy perennial, with deeply divided, coarsely toothed, green leaves. Plumes of tiny, off-white flowers appear in late summer and autumn. Prefers moist soil. Height 4–5 ft (1.2–1.5 m). Spread 20 in (50 cm).

CARE
Cut back to within 6 in (15 cm) of ground level in spring. Prune again after flowering if required.

A. abrotanum (SOUTHERNWOOD)
Hardy, semievergreen, shrubby perennial. Leaves are aromatic and gray-green. It is often nonflowering in cool areas. Height 3 ft (1 m). Spread 1–2 ft (30–60 cm).

A. dracunculus
(TARRAGON, FRENCH TARRAGON)
Frost-hardy, creeping perennial with smooth, slender, midgreen leaves, and a mint-anise aroma. Tiny, globose, green-white flowers are produced in clusters in late summer, but often fail to develop in cool areas. Height 18 in–3 ft (45 cm–1 m) Spread 12–15 in (30–38 cm).

A. annua (SWEET ANNIE)
Giant, frost-hardy annual with bright green, deeply divided, saw-toothed leaves. Tiny yellow flowers are produced in loose clusters in summer. Height 5–10 ft (1.5–3 m). Spread 3–5 ft (1–1.5 m).

A. ludoviciana 'SILVER QUEEN' (WESTERN MUGWORT, WHITE SAGE)
Bushy, hardy perennial with jagged, silver leaves up to 4 in (10 cm) long, and with plumes of yellow-gray flowers in summer and autumn. It spreads rapidly by means of creeping rhizomes. Height 30 in (75 cm). Spread indefinite.

8

Borago officinalis
BORAGE
BORAGINACEAE

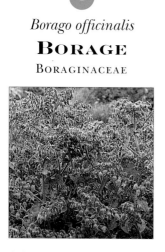

Fresh borage flowers and leaves have been added to wine and salads since classical times. The seeds contain an oil, rich in linolenic acid, which has a similar effect to evening primrose oil.

HABIT Hardy annual with coarsely hairy, cucumber-scented leaves, and bright blue star-shaped flowers throughout the summer.

HEIGHT 1–3 ft (30 cm–1 m).

SPREAD 6–12 in (15–30 cm).

REMARKS The bright blue flowers of borage make a brilliant contrast to orange pot marigolds (*Calendula officinalis*), California poppies (*Eschscholzia californica*), and corn poppies (*Papaver rhoeas*).

CARE

Sow borage *in situ*, since it forms a stout taproot and will not transplant well. Thin seedlings to 18 in (45 cm) apart. Self-sows in most gardens. Plants tend to flop, and usually need staking. The bristly foliage can cause skin irritation.

FLOWERS
Bright blue, five-petaled, and star-shaped, fading to white in the center, and with conspicuous black stamen tips.

LEAVES
Midgreen, oval, and pointed, with a rough, bristly texture. They smell and taste of cucumber.

SEEDS
Relatively large nutlets, 0.2–0.3 in (5–8 mm) in length, and almost black. Viable for several years if kept in a cool, dry place.

STEM
Stout, hollow, and clad in bristly white hairs. It is upright at first, branching and leaning as it develops.

VARIATIONS

_B. s._ 'SUFFRUTICOSA'
A dwarf variant with glossy,
bright green foliage. Height
and spread 30 in (75 cm).

_B. s._ 'ELEGANTISSIMA'
This has small leaves with
white margins. Height 6 ft
(2 m). Spread 3–5 ft
(1–1.5 m).

Buxus sempervirens
BOXWOOD
BUXACEAE

Boxwood is very long-living and
slow-growing, with a dense, neat
foliage. It has has been a favorite
shrub for hedging and topiary since
Roman times. Though very
poisonous, it was once used to treat
feverish illnesses, such as malaria.
HABIT Hardy, evergreen shrub.
Pale green, honey-scented flowers
in spring, followed by small, oval,
three-horned fruits.
HEIGHT 6–15 ft (2–5 m).
SPREAD 4–6 ft (1.2–2 m).
REMARKS Unrivaled as a shrub for
dwarf hedging in knot gardens and
as a clipped specimen shrub. Use the
formal shapes of boxwood topiary
at focal points in a garden.

CARE
Boxwood is hardy to –10°F
(–23°C) but prefers higher
winter temperatures.
In cold areas, protect
specimen shrubs with
a layer of insulating
material. Trim hedges
and topiary to shape in
summer. Reduce the
unpleasant smell of cut
foliage by trimming after
rain or watering. Repot
young potted plants in
spring, or top-dress if in
final container. Handling
boxwood foliage may
cause dermatitis.

LEAVES
_Glossy and dark
green. They reach
0.5–1.5 in
(1–3 cm) in
length._

Calendula officinalis
POT MARIGOLD
COMPOSITAE

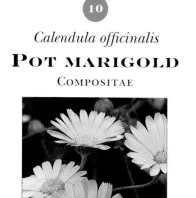

This colorful, versatile herb is very easy to grow, and blooms continuously, providing an almost year-round supply of petals for coloring and flavoring in the kitchen, or for simple skin preparations.

HABIT Hardy, long-lived, aromatic annual with a bushy habit.

HEIGHT 20–28 in (50–70 cm).

SPREAD 20–28 in (50–70 cm).

REMARKS Plant pot marigolds with borage (*Borago officinalis*) and cornflowers (*Centaurea cyanea*), or create contrast with a background of bronze fennel (*Foeniculum vulgare* 'Purpureum') or purple elder (*Sambucus nigra* 'Guincho Purple').

SEED HEAD
This contains the seeds, which can easily be collected for growing the following year.

LEAVES
Light green in color, with a narrow-oblong shape. They reach 2–7 in (5–17 cm) in length.

SEEDS
Light brown and C-shaped. They can be up to 0.2 in (5 mm) in length.

FLOWERS
Yellow-orange ray florets (a source of yellow dye) with central yellow-orange to brown disks.

STEM
Branched and more or less upright.

CARE
Sow in autumn for very early flowers, and again in spring for blooming throughout summer and autumn. Removing dead flower heads prolongs flowering and prevents excessive self-seeding.

FLOWERS
Terminal clusters of pink to lilac, tubular, two-lipped flowers, about 0.4 in (1 cm) long, and opening in succession.

Cedronella canariensis
BALM OF GILEAD
LABIATAE

This is an attractive, aromatic plant for potpourris and herb teas, but it is more often grown for its exotic name. True balm of Gilead is a medicinal resin, collected from a desert shrub, *Balsamodendron opobalsamum*, balsam fir (*Abies balsamea*), and various poplars.

HABIT Tender, shrubby perennial with strongly scented leaves.

HEIGHT 5 ft (1.5 m).

SPREAD 3 ft (1 m).

REMARKS Grow in frost-free gardens, or in pots for the conservatory or patio, beside scented geraniums (*Pelargonium* species), which have similarly interesting aromas.

LEAVES
Trifoliate, and up to 4 in (10 cm) in length, with slender-oblong, tapering leaflets, serrated margins, and a cedar-lemon aroma.

STEM
Square in cross-section, and ridged with a rough texture.

CARE
Cut back hard in spring to encourage new shoots from the base, and lightly again after flowering. Mulch with well-rotted manure or compost in spring. Repot young plants, or top-dress plants in large pots in spring.

Centaurea cyanus

CORNFLOWER

COMPOSITAE

Cornflowers are favorite garden annuals, and an easily grown herb that benefits skin, hair, and eyes.

HABIT Tall, slender, hardy annual, with bright blue (occasionally white, pink, or purple) flowers on long stalks in summer.

HEIGHT 8 in–3 ft (20 cm–1 m).

SPREAD 6–12 in (15–30 cm).

REMARKS Grow vivid blue cornflowers with scarlet poppies (*Papaver rhoeas*), their natural companions in the wild. For added realism, combine the seeds with a packet of ornamental grasses. They also look good with pot marigolds (*Calendula officinalis*) and evening primroses (*Oenothera biennis*).

CARE

Sow in autumn for early flowers the following year, or in spring for summer blooms. For a prolonged flowering period, sow every three weeks from early spring to autumn. They do not transplant well, so sow *in situ* and thin to 9 in (23 cm) apart. They are naturally erect among other plants, but may need staking when exposed. Regular deadheading will extend the flowering period.

FLOWERS
The radiating outer florets are tubular and deeply lobed, surrounding smaller central florets. Flower heads last well in water and retain color when dried.

VARIATION

C. c. 'FLORENCE SERIES'
A compact variety with blue, pink, carmine, and white flowers.
Height 15–18 in (38–45 cm).
Spread 6–12 in (15–30 cm).

STEM
Long, slender, and grooved, with many wiry branches.

LEAVES
Linear and slender in shape, these are gray-green in color, and cottony.

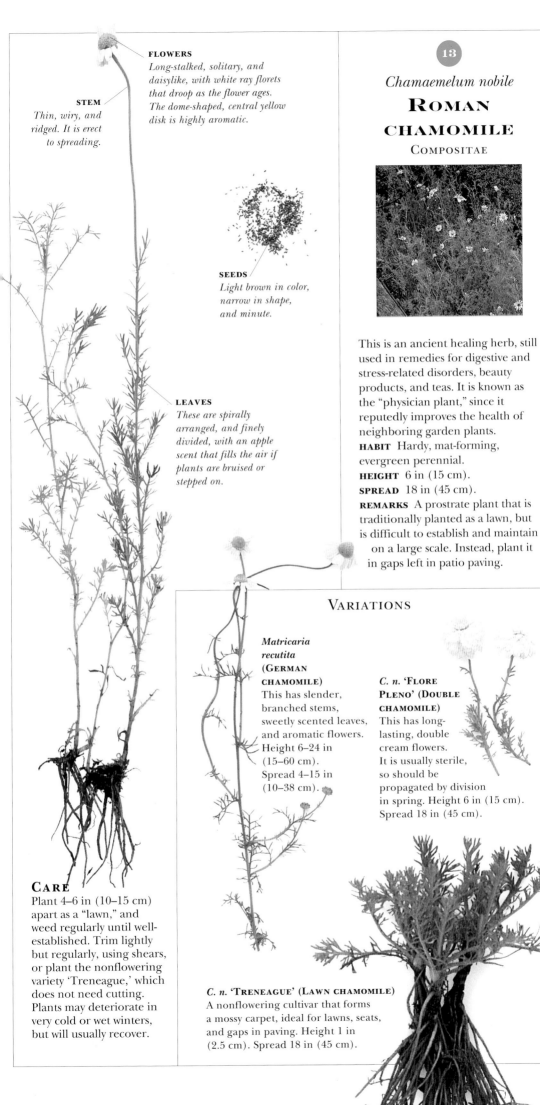

FLOWERS
Long-stalked, solitary, and daisylike, with white ray florets that droop as the flower ages. The dome-shaped, central yellow disk is highly aromatic.

STEM
Thin, wiry, and ridged. It is erect to spreading.

SEEDS
Light brown in color, narrow in shape, and minute.

LEAVES
These are spirally arranged, and finely divided, with an apple scent that fills the air if plants are bruised or stepped on.

13

Chamaemelum nobile

ROMAN CHAMOMILE

COMPOSITAE

This is an ancient healing herb, still used in remedies for digestive and stress-related disorders, beauty products, and teas. It is known as the "physician plant," since it reputedly improves the health of neighboring garden plants.

HABIT Hardy, mat-forming, evergreen perennial.

HEIGHT 6 in (15 cm).

SPREAD 18 in (45 cm).

REMARKS A prostrate plant that is traditionally planted as a lawn, but is difficult to establish and maintain on a large scale. Instead, plant it in gaps left in patio paving.

VARIATIONS

Matricaria recutita (GERMAN CHAMOMILE)
This has slender, branched stems, sweetly scented leaves, and aromatic flowers. Height 6–24 in (15–60 cm). Spread 4–15 in (10–38 cm).

C. n. 'FLORE PLENO' (DOUBLE CHAMOMILE)
This has long-lasting, double cream flowers. It is usually sterile, so should be propagated by division in spring. Height 6 in (15 cm). Spread 18 in (45 cm).

CARE
Plant 4–6 in (10–15 cm) apart as a "lawn," and weed regularly until well-established. Trim lightly but regularly, using shears, or plant the nonflowering variety 'Treneague,' which does not need cutting. Plants may deteriorate in very cold or wet winters, but will usually recover.

C. n. 'TRENEAGUE' (LAWN CHAMOMILE)
A nonflowering cultivar that forms a mossy carpet, ideal for lawns, seats, and gaps in paving. Height 1 in (2.5 cm). Spread 18 in (45 cm).

Digitalis purpurea
FOXGLOVE
SCROPHULARIACEAE

This is a popular, but poisonous, garden plant, grown for its elegant, one-sided spires of tubular flowers. It is the source of important heart drugs, such as digitoxin.

HABIT Tall, hardy biennial with tall spikes of flowers in summer.
HEIGHT 3–6 ft (1–2 m).
SPREAD 1–2 ft (30–60 cm).
REMARKS Grow foxgloves among trees and shrubs, at the backs of borders, or where they are illuminated by shafts of early morning or evening sun. Their poisonous foliage is easily confused with that of comfrey (*Symphytum officinale*). Position them out of reach of children and pets.

FLOWERS
Natural variation produces occasional white-flowered plants.

LEAVES
Oval to slender in shape, they have a soft, thin, and slightly wrinkled texture, with a blunt tip and finely serrated margins.

CARE
Foxglove seed is very tiny and needs light to germinate. For best results, mix with sand and scatter thinly *in situ.* It will self-sow in most gardens, especially on slightly acid soils.

FLOWERS
Racemes of 20 to 80 purple-pink, tubular flowers, with pale, purple-spotted insides.

STEM
This is usually solitary, and has a smooth texture.

D. lanata
(WOOLLY FOXGLOVE)
Hardy biennial or short-lived perennial, with a purple-tinged stem and narrow leaves.
Height 3 ft (1 m).
Spread 12 in (24 cm).

D. lutea
(YELLOW FOXGLOVE)
Hardy perennial, with smooth, pointed leaves and cream flowers.
Height 30 in (75 cm).
Spread 12 in (30 cm).

FLOWERS
Honey-scented daisies up to 4 in (10 cm) across, with purple-pink ray florets, and conical, dark orange-brown centers.

Echinacea purpurea
PURPLE CONEFLOWER
COMPOSITAE

Purple coneflowers are both beautiful and useful. Once regarded as a cure-all, they are now known to stimulate the immune system and clear toxins from the body. Their magnificent flowers give glowing color to the herb garden.

HABIT Hardy, rhizomatous perennial. Large, scented flowers in summer and early autumn.

HEIGHT 4 ft (1.2 m).

SPREAD 18 in (45 cm).

REMARKS A tall, colorful border plant, effective against herbs such as bronze fennel (*Foeniculum vulgare* 'Purpureum') and purple elder (*Sambucus nigra* 'Guincho Purple').

CARE
For best results, feed with well-rotted manure or compost in spring. Stake plants securely, early in the season, to prevent flopping as flowering begins. Remove dead flowers regularly to prolong display. Cut back to ground level when foliage has died off in autumn.

LEAVES
These have a slender, oval shape, and are shallow-toothed with a rough texture. They taper to a point, and are up to 6 in (15 cm) long.

VARIATION

E. angustifolia
(NARROW-LEAVED CONEFLOWER)
Very similar to *E. purpurea*, but slightly taller, with slender leaves and drooping, narrower ray florets. Height 5 ft (1.5 m). Spread 18 in (45 cm).

16

Eschscholzia californica

CALIFORNIA POPPY

PAPAVERACEAE

This easily grown annual is the state flower of California. It is a mildly sedative herb, used by native North Americans for toothache. **HABIT** Hardy, upright to sprawling annual with a long taproot. Vivid flowers of yellow and orange all summer, followed by ribbed capsules up to 4 in (10 cm) long. **HEIGHT** 8–24 in (20–60 cm). **SPREAD** 6–12 in (15–30 cm). **REMARKS** Emphasize the waxy foliage of the California poppy by planting with rue (*Ruta graveolens* 'Jackman's Blue') and sorrel (*Rumex scutatus* 'Silver Leaf').

STEM
Slender, brittle, and either upright or spreading.

CARE
Flowers best in dry, sandy, sun-baked conditions. Sow in succession from spring to early summer for a long period of color. In warm, dry areas, seed may also be sown in late summer for flowers the following spring. Does not transplant successfully; sow *in situ* and thin to 15 cm (6 in) apart. Self-sows in most gardens.

FLOWERS
Solitary and yellow to orange in color. Between 2 and 3 in (5–8 cm) across, with four petals that curl up in cloudy weather. For cutting, pick just before opening.

LEAVES
Smooth, blue-green, and finely cut, with long stalks and a waxy bloom. Easily damaged, and both leaves and stems contain watery latex.

SEEDS
*Dark brown, narrow,
and pointed. Up to
0.1 in (3 mm) in length,
with a tuft of hairs.*

CARE
Stake in early summer
to prevent wind damage
as flowering approaches.
Cut down dead stems
in winter. Mulch with
well-rotted manure
or compost in spring.

Eupatorium purpureum
JOE-PYE WEED
COMPOSITAE

This stately, late-flowering,
medicinal herb is suited to the
backs of large borders. It is named
after Jopi, a native North American
who used it to cure typhus.
HABIT Hardy perennial with dense
clusters of pink flowers in late
summer and autumn.
HEIGHT 4–10 ft (1.2–3 m).
SPREAD 2–3 ft (60 cm–1 m).
REMARKS Plant this tall herb with
bold angelica (*Angelica*) and
sunflowers (*Helianthus annuus*), or
beside shrubby herbs such as elder
(*Sambucus nigra*) and Chinese
chaste tree (*Vitex negundo*).
Try also near purple elder
(*Sambucus nigra* 'Guincho Purple').

FLOWERS
*Pale pink to purple-
pink (occasionally
yellow-green or
white), appearing
in rounded clusters.*

LEAVES
*Whorls of three to six oval,
finely toothed leaves,
which have a vanilla
scent when crushed.*

STEM
*Stout, upright,
and maroon or
tinged purple at
the nodes.*

VARIATION

**E. cannabinum
(HEMP
AGRIMONY)**
Hardy perennial
with downy
stems.
Height 1–4 ft
(30 cm–
1.2 m).
Spread
1–2 ft (30–
60 cm).

18

Foeniculum vulgare
FENNEL
UMBELLIFERAE

Fennel has been grown as an herb and a vegetable since classical times. All parts are edible and beneficial, containing an essential oil that improves digestion. It is also indispensable as a garden plant, with delightful feathery foliage.

HABIT Hardy perennial with stout stems and glossy leaves.

HEIGHT 6 ft (2 m).

SPREAD 18 in (45 cm).

REMARKS An outstanding border plant because of its stiffly upright stems, which rarely need staking. Plant beside other tall, yellow-flowered herbs, such as evening primroses (*Oenothera biennis*) and mullein (*Verbascum thapsus*).

CARE
Grow from seed in autumn or spring. Keep well away from dill (*Anethum graveolens*), since they hybridize easily. Though hardy, fennel dislikes cold, damp winters, and may need protecting with a layer of insulating material.

VARIATION

**F. v. 'PURPUREUM'
(BRONZE FENNEL)**
A favorite cultivar with rich brown foliage. Comes true from seed, and usually self-sows. Hardier in cold, damp areas than the species. Height 4–5 ft (1.2–1.5 m). Spread 18 in (45 cm).

LEAVES
Broadly triangular in outline, glossy, and anise-scented. Up to 12 in (30 cm) long, and divided into threadlike segments. The leaf stalk clasps the stem.

FLOWERS
Tiny and dull yellow, appearing in aromatic, flat-topped clusters.

STEM
Erect, shiny, finely lined, and hollow. It branches at the onset of flowering.

SEEDS
Oval in shape, green-brown, with an anise flavor, and a ribbed texture. They measure 0.15–0.2 in (4 to 6 mm).

VARIATION

F. v. 'VARIEGATA'
This cultivar has cream-
edged leaves.
Height 10 in (25 cm).
Spread 8 in (20 cm).

SEEDS
*Very small and tear-
shaped. They are glossy
and pale brown in color,
and are embedded in the
skin of the fruit.*

LEAVES
*Trifoliate, with
oval, deeply veined
and toothed leaflets
up to 2.4 in
(6 cm) long. When
thoroughly dried,
they can be used in
herbal tea mixtures.*

FLOWERS
*White, five-petaled,
about 0.2 in (0.5 cm)
across, and with
yellow centers.*

19

Fragaria vesca
WILD STRAWBERRY
ROSACEAE

Strawberry plants have always been
used as household remedies for
skin problems and other ailments.
Fruits of wild strawberries are
smaller than those of cultivated
varieties, but are very aromatic.
HABIT Hardy perennial with long
runners, which root where the
leaves and stem join. Flowers
followed by bright red, oval fruits.
HEIGHT 10 in (25 cm).
SPREAD 8 in (20 cm).
REMARKS A tolerant, easily grown,
useful herb, which makes excellent
groundcover between taller
perennials and beneath shrubs.

STEM
*Slender, wiry, and
often red-tinged.*

CARE
May be invasive in some
gardens, so remove excess
runners as they appear.
Fruits are often hidden under
the foliage, and are usually
safe from birds, but may need
protection from slugs. Easily
propagated from plantlets
at the ends of runners.

Galega officinalis

GOAT'S RUE

LEGUMINOSAE

This interesting medicinal herb and beautiful border plant has been renowned since ancient times for improving milk yields in cows. The fresh juice is also used to coagulate milk for cheesemaking. Its scientific name comes from the Greek word *gala*, meaning milk.

HABIT Hardy, bushy perennial, flowering in summer.

HEIGHT 3–5 ft (1–1.5 m).

SPREAD 2–3 ft (60 cm–1 m).

REMARKS Ideal in a mixed border with predominantly red, pink, and purple coloring. Effective with roses (*Rosa*), purple coneflowers (*Echinacea purpurea*), and opium poppies (*Papaver somniferum*).

LEAVES
These are smooth, midgreen, and divided into pairs of oblong leaflets, about 2 in (5 cm) long, on either side of the leaf stalk.

FLOWERS
Lavender to pink-and-white pea flowers in long-stalked racemes, which appear where the leaves meet the stem.

STEM
More or less upright, branched, hollow, and fairly weak.

CARE

Easy and fast-growing from seed or divisions. Sow seed in the open ground in spring, and separate seedlings when large enough to handle. Plant among roses to help support stems, or stake mature plants early in the growing season to prevent flopping as flowering begins.

20

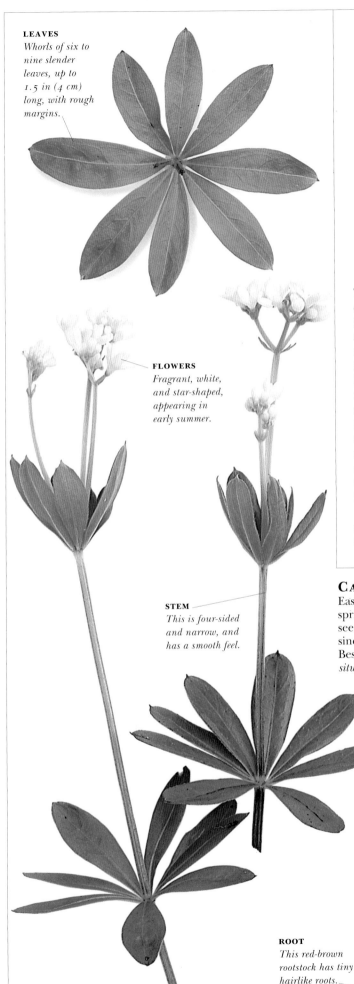

LEAVES
Whorls of six to nine slender leaves, up to 1.5 in (4 cm) long, with rough margins.

FLOWERS
Fragrant, white, and star-shaped, appearing in early summer.

STEM
This is four-sided and narrow, and has a smooth feel.

ROOT
This red-brown rootstock has tiny hairlike roots.

Galium odoratum

SWEET WOODRUFF

RUBIACEAE

This pretty woodland herb contains coumarin, which develops the sweet smell of new-mown hay as it dries. It is traditionally used to flavor white wine as a drink for May Day in Germany, giving it the common name *Maiwein*.

HABIT Hardy perennial with slender, wiry, creeping rhizomes.

HEIGHT 20 in (50 cm).

SPREAD Indefinite.

REMARKS A good herb for ground-cover in shady borders, especially under trees and shrubs, or with larger herbs, such as angelica (*Angelica*). Dies down in winter, so useful with spring bulbs that flower before new shoots appear.

CARE

Easily propagated by division in spring or autumn, but tricky from seed. Germination may be erratic, since the seeds need exposure to cold. Best results are obtained by sowing *in situ*, enriching the soil with leaf mold. May be invasive in some gardens. Control by removing excess runners, or by planting among large, vigorous herbs. Mulch with leaf mold in early spring.

Hedera helix
ENGLISH IVY
ARALIACEAE

Sacred to Bacchus, or Dionysius, god of wine, ivy was believed to prevent intoxication if bound to the brow or steeped in wine. This poisonous herb is used today in preparations for skin problems.

HABIT Hardy, climbing, or carpeting evergreen with roots appearing all along the stems.

HEIGHT 30–100 ft (10–30 m).

SPREAD 15 ft (5 m).

REMARKS Ivy is a tolerant plant that thrives in most conditions, including heavy shade, both indoors and out. It is traditionally planted as groundcover under large trees, but may cause damage if allowed to climb the trunks.

STEM
Brittle, and densely clad in roots that cling to the climbing surface.

FLOWERS
Yellow-green flowers, rich in nectar. They appear late in the year, and attract bees on mild days. Produced only toward the tops of mature, nonclimbing plants.

LEAVES
Dark green, often with paler veins, sometimes tinged purple. Three to five triangular lobes in young specimens, becoming whole and angular-oval in shape on flowering stems.

FRUITS
Poisonous, globose, black berries, 0.2–0.3 in (6–8 mm) in diameter.

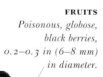

CARE
Trained plants need to have shoots tied in regularly before the stems toughen and become brittle. Prune to shape in spring, and again in summer to control new growths. Ivy stems thicken with age, so check for structural damage if growing on walls.

SEEDS
*The shells are commonly
striped gray-black and
white, and contain
kernels rich in protein,
oil, vitamins, and
minerals.*

CARE
Sow in spring, in
the open ground,
thinning to 12–18 in
(30–45 cm) apart, or
in pots, setting out
when about 6 in
(15 cm) high. Stake
plants, using sturdy
stakes or poles,
before flowers
develop.

SEED HEAD
*The seeds are edible
and are arranged in
concentric spirals.*

Helianthus annuus
SUNFLOWER
COMPOSITAE

This cheerful, familiar garden
annual is grown commercially for
its edible seeds. It is an important
source of polyunsaturated oil, and
is also used in aromatherapy.
HABIT Tall, giant, tender annual
with stout stems and rough leaves.
Large, daisylike flowers in summer.
HEIGHT 10 ft (3 m) or more.
SPREAD 12–18 in (30–45 cm).
REMARKS Sunflowers turn to face
the sun, so consider direction when
planting them. They are especially
effective in groups against a wall or
fence, which helps protect against
wind, or at the back of a border.
Seeds may not ripen in areas with
cold, damp autumns.

LEAVES
*Alternately arranged, heart-
shaped, 4–12 in (10–30 cm)
long and 4–8 in (10–20 cm)
wide, with toothed margins
and a rough texture.*

FLOWERS
*Large, drooping, up to 12 in
(30 cm) across, with brown disk
florets and yellow ray florets.*

STEM
*Stout, erect,
usually
unbranched,
and hairy.*

24

Helichrysum italicum
CURRY PLANT
COMPOSITAE

This silver-leaved herb fills the air with an intriguing smell of curry, especially after rain. The leaves have a bitter flavor and cannot be used to make curries, but may be added in very small amounts to soups and stews.

HABIT Evergreen, frost-hardy subshrub with clusters of button flowers in summer.

HEIGHT 2 ft (60 cm).

SPREAD 3 ft (1 m).

REMARKS Grow as a low, informal hedge in the herb garden, or plant at the foot of tall, woolly mullein (*Verbascum thapsus*). Flower heads dry well for floral arrangements and potpourris.

FLOWERS
Mustard yellow, and curry-scented. Formed in broad clusters, 1–2 in (2.5–5 cm) across, on long, silvery stalks.

VARIATION

H. i. **SUBSP.**
microphyllum
Useful for containers, rock gardens, and edges.
Height 10 in (25 cm).
Spread 6 in (15 cm).

CARE
Dislikes cold, wet winters, so plant in a sunny, sheltered position, with good drainage. In severe winters, protect with a layer of insulating material. Cut back hard to old wood in spring, since curry plants often look bedraggled by the end of winter.

LEAVES
Long, silver-gray, and needlelike.

STEM
White-felted shoots, which are woody at the base.

CARE

Avoid planting next to paths and seats, since rough stems may be a hazard. Remove dead stems in winter. Mulch with well-rotted manure or compost in spring, and tie in new growths regularly. Propagate only by division or cuttings of female plants, since males are less ornamental and useful. Branches of female flowers dry well for decorations and arrangements.

STEM
Climbing, twining clockwise, and bristly. It may cause abrasion or irritation to skin.

FLOWERS
Tiny, with males in clusters, and females in conelike spikes (strobiles) that have a resinous scent.

Humulus lupulus

HOPS

CANNABIDACEAE

This climber was first used in brewing in about the 9th century. The flavor of beer is derived from the female flowers, which also have a sedative effect.

HABIT Vigorous, hardy climber with deeply lobed leaves. Male and female flowers are borne on separate plants in summer.

HEIGHT 10–20 ft (3–6 m).

SPREAD 10–20 ft (3–6 m).

REMARKS Makes an ornamental curtain of foliage as background for the herb garden, covering fences and walls within a season. Dies down completely in winter. May also be grown over arches and pergolas to give height.

VARIATION

H. l. 'AUREUS' (GOLDEN HOPS)
This has yellow-green foliage and does not scorch in the sun. Height and spread 10–20 ft (3–6 m).

LEAVES
Long-stalked, broadly heart-shaped, 4–6 in (10–15 cm) across, with three to five lobes, and coarsely toothed margins.

STROBILE
The flowers on the female plant are found under soft, papery bracts in a strobile such as this.

Hyssopus officinalis
HYSSOP
LABIATAE

This is an ancient herb, mentioned in the Old Testament for purification, and used by herbalists to treat bronchial infections. Its name comes from the Hebrew word *ezob*, meaning holy herb.
HABIT Hardy, semievergreen perennial with aromatic leaves. Spikes of flowers are produced in late summer.
HEIGHT 18–24 in (45–60 cm).
SPREAD 2–3 ft (60 cm–1 m).
REMARKS One of the best late-flowering herbs for borders, attracting bees and butterflies to its nectar-rich flowers. It may also be grown as a low hedge in knot gardens, or as edging.

SEEDS
Brown, tear-shaped, and 0.1 in (3 mm) long.

CARE
Trim hedges lightly, and cut back specimen plants hard in spring. To make a hedge, set young plants 9–12 in (23–30 cm) apart in spring, and pinch out the growing tips to encourage bushiness.

LEAVES
Narrow, almost blunt, and up to 1 in (2.5 cm) in length. They have a bitter, sage-mint aroma.

FLOWERS
Whorls of tubular, two-lipped, purple-blue flowers, with narrow, tapering bracts.

VARIATIONS

H. o. 'ALBUS'
The white-flowered hyssop is lovely in white borders. Height 18–24 in (45–60 cm). Spread 2–3 ft (60 cm–1 m).

H.o. FORMA roseus
The pink-flowered form of hyssop combines well with gray-leaved artemisias. Height 18–24 in (45–60 cm). Spread 2–3 ft (60 cm–1 m).

H. o. 'NETHERFIELD'
A new variety, with gold-variegated foliage. Height 18 in (45 cm). Spread 2 ft (60 cm).

VARIATIONS

**L. n. 'ANGUSTIFOLIA'
(WILLOW-LEAF BAY)**
This variety is hardier
than the species, and has
wavy-edged leaves.
Height 10–50 ft (3–15 m).
Spread 30 ft (10 m).

**L. n. 'AUREA'
(GOLDEN BAY)**
This is best grown
unclipped to display the
golden foliage.
Height 10–50 ft (3–15 m).
Spread 30 ft (10 m).

LEAVES
*Narrowly oval, olive green,
and tapering to a point.
They have a thin, leathery
texture, and a smooth,
shiny surface.*

CARE
Give a sheltered spot in
cold areas; young plants
(under two years old)
are very sensitive to cold.
Foliage may be damaged
by cold winds, as well as
frost. If in danger,
protect the whole
plant with a layer
of insulating
material.

27

Laurus nobilis
BAY
LAURACEAE

Sprigs of bay were woven into
crowns in Roman times, and this
tradition gave the plant its name –
Laurus, meaning praise, and *nobilis*,
meaning noble or excellent. The
handsome, fragrant leaves are
indispensable for flavoring food.
HABIT Dense, frost-hardy,
evergreen shrub or small tree.
Clusters of small, creamy yellow
flowers in spring and summer.
 HEIGHT 10–50 ft (3–15 m).
 SPREAD 30 ft (10 m).
 REMARKS Bay can be cut
 into formal shapes, such as
standards and topiaries, to give
focal points in herb gardens. They
make good subjects for containers.

STEM
*Densely branched and woody.
Suckers appear regularly at the base
of the plant. If detached carefully
with some root, they can be used
for propagation.*

FRUITS
*Rounded,
shiny, purple-
green berries,
which ripen to
black. They are
not edible, but
yield an oil used
to make soap.*

Lavandula angustifolia
LAVENDER
LABIATAE

No herb garden is complete without lavenders, with their subtle colors and invigorating fragrance.
HABIT Small, evergreen shrub with narrow, woolly, gray-green leaves and a distinctive fragrance. Spikes of small purple flowers are borne on long stalks in summer.
HEIGHT 2–3 ft (60 cm–1 m).
SPREAD 2–3 ft (60 cm–1 m).
REMARKS This lavender and its many varieties are effective as dwarf, informal hedges, and in borders, having a neat, rounded habit. To make a hedge, plant 9–12 in (23–30 cm) apart in early autumn or spring, pinching out growing tips to encourage bushiness.

L. 'SAWYER'S'
A hybrid lavender that forms a distinctively broad, dome-shaped bush, with gray leaves and large, lavender-blue spikes, opening to purple. Suitable for hedging or as a specimen plant.
Height 18–27 in (45–68 cm).
Spread 3.5 ft (1.1 m).

L. a. 'HIDCOTE'
One of the best varieties for hedging, with a compact, erect habit. Leaves are neat, gray, and strongly scented, with deep purple flowers in dense spikes up to 2 in (5 cm) long.
Height 1–2 ft (30–60 cm).
Spread 12 in (30 cm).

L. a. 'ROSEA'
The classic pink lavender. Later varieties, such as 'Loddon Pink' and 'Jean Davis,' are virtually indistinguishable in flower color, habit, and perfume.
Height 9–18 in (23–45 cm).
Spread 12–18 in (30–45 cm).

L. a. 'NANA ALBA' (DWARF WHITE LAVENDER)
This tiny, compact lavender has an upright habit, silver-gray leaves, and white flowers. It is ideal for rock gardens, containers, white borders, and edging, or for a miniature hedge.
Height 6–12 in (15–30 cm).
Spread 6–18 in (15–45 cm).

L. a. 'MUNSTEAD'
A compact, early-flowering lavender, with small leaves and strongly scented, blue flowers. Seed-raised plants are not recommended for hedging, because they may not be uniform in size, habit, or flower color. Height 12–18 in (30–45 cm). Spread 30 in (75 cm).

L. lanata
Woolly lavender has white-felted leaves, and spikes of lilac flowers.
Height 2 ft (60 cm).
Spread 20 in (50 cm).

VARIATIONS

L. stoechas
(FRENCH LAVENDER)
A frost-hardy, dense, and
bushy shrub with narrow,
light green leaves,
and very dark purple
flowers in summer,
topped by purple-
white bracts. Given
a dry, sheltered
position, it is often
hardy in cold areas.
Height and spread
1–3 ft (30 cm–1 m).

CARE
Trim hedges and
cut back specimen
plants in spring to
maintain a compact
habit. Remove
dead flower spikes
and trim lightly
when flowering
has finished.

L. s. SUBSP. *pedunculata*
(SPANISH LAVENDER)
This showy, frost-hardy
lavender is larger all
over than *L. stoechas*,
with much longer flower
stalks. It is good for
warm, dry positions.
Height and spread
30 in (75 cm).

L. dentata (FRINGED LAVENDER)
A half-hardy lavender with woolly stems and
narrow, gray-green leaves, which have woolly
undersides. Dark purple flowers are borne in
spikes. Height and spread 2–3 ft (60 cm–1 m).

29

Melissa officinalis
LEMON BALM
LABIATAE

Originally grown as a bee plant to encourage swarms into empty hives, *Melissa* gets its name from the Greek word for honeybee. It is now popular as an ingredient of herb teas and potpourris, because of its lemon scent and calming effects.

HABIT Hardy, upright perennial. Insignificant, off-white flowers appear in summer.

HEIGHT 12–32 in (30–80 cm).

SPREAD 12–18 in (30–45 cm).

REMARKS A useful herb for shady corners, at its best in spring before the stems elongate for flowering. Try beside the ferny leaves of sweet cicely (*Myrrhis odorata*), or reedlike chives (*Allium schoenoprasum*).

CARE

Mulch with well-rotted manure or compost in spring. Cut back to within 6 in (15 cm) of ground level after flowering to encourage a second flush of new growth, which will remain in good condition until the first frosts. Remove dead stems just above ground level in winter.

VARIATION

M. o. 'AUREA'
(GOLDEN LEMON BALM)
Good for damp, shady corners. Height 1–2 ft (30–60 cm). Spread 12–18 in (30–45 cm).

LEAVES
Oval in shape, bright green, and arranged oppositely, with a slightly hairy, strongly veined surface, and neatly scalloped to toothed margins. They measure 1.1–3 in (3–8 cm) and have a delightful lemon scent, which diminishes on drying.

STEM
Erect, light green, and four-angled, branching and elongating as flower buds are formed.

SEEDS
Each seed case contains four shiny, dark brown nutlets, 0.04 in (1 mm) long. They are tear-shaped and have white tips.

42

VARIATIONS

M. spicata
'MOROCCAN'
(MOROCCAN SPEARMINT)
A favorite culinary variety.
Height 1–3 ft (30 cm–1 m).
Spread indefinite.

M. suaveolens
'VARIEGATA'
(PINEAPPLE
MINT)
This
ornamental
mint
has soft,
hairy
leaves.
Height
16 in–3 ft
(40 cm–1 m).
Spread indefinite.

M. aquatica **(WATERMINT)**
Variable, creeping
perennial with red-purple
stems. Height
1–3 ft
(30cm–1m).
Spread
indefinite.

M. x gracilis
'VARIEGATA'
(GINGER MINT)
An attractive mint
with yellow-
streaked leaves,
and a subtle
flavor, with
a hint of fruit
and spice.
Height
1–3 ft
(30cm–1m).
Spread indefinite.

CARE
Mints are notoriously
invasive, so plant in
containers, or sink into
the ground in a large
pot or strong plastic
bag to restrict spread.
Repot annually when
dormant, using rich soil
mix and discarding all
but a few short sections
of rhizome. In the open
ground, remove excess
runners as they appear.
Cut down dead stems
in autumn. Mulch with
well-rotted manure
or compost in spring.

LEAVES
*Bright green and
narrowly oval, with
a deeply veined
surface and regularly
toothed margins.*

STEM
*Slender, upright,
and branched. It is
square in cross-section.*

30

Mentha spicata
SPEARMINT
LABIATAE

Mint is one of the oldest existing
plant names. As the world's most
popular flavor, it is used in many
foods, drinks, and medicines.
HABIT Hardy, creeping perennial,
whose leaves have a classic aroma.
Tiny lilac to pink or white flowers
are produced in a spike in summer.
HEIGHT 1–3 ft (30 cm–1 m).
SPREAD Indefinite.
REMARKS Plant near large, vigorous
herbs that also enjoy rich, moist
soil. Examples include sweet
cicely (*Myrrhis odorata*), angelica
(*Angelica archangelica*), and bee
balm (*Monarda didyma*).
Mint flowers attract flies, so avoid
planting them near seats.

43

Monarda didyma
BEE BALM
LABIATAE

This North American woodland herb is famous as the source of Oswego tea, made by colonists to replace Indian tea following the Boston Tea Party in 1773. It has a similar aroma to the bergamot orange (*Citrus bergamia*), which is used to flavor Earl Grey tea.

HABIT Hardy perennial with sweetly perfumed leaves, and bright red flowers in summer and autumn.

HEIGHT 16 in–4 ft (40 cm–1.2 m).

SPREAD 1–2 ft (30–60 cm).

REMARKS An outstanding border plant, given suitable conditions. It is best planted in clumps of three to six, and looks good with mints (*Mentha* species).

LEAVES
Oval in shape, up to 4 in (10 cm) long, and tapering to a point, with serrated margins and a reddish midrib. They have a sweet aroma, reminiscent of citrus and eau de cologne, which is strongest in young foliage.

***M. d.* 'BLUE STOCKING'**
Purple-flowered, and pretty in mixed clumps.
Height 3 ft (1 m).
Spread 18 in (45 cm).

***M. d.* 'CROFTWAY PINK'**
Try planting with mauve-flowered herbs, such as mints. Height 3 ft (1 m).
Spread 18 in (45 cm).

M. fistulosa
Likes alkaline conditions.
Height 4 ft (1.2 m).
Spread 18 in (45 cm).

FLOWERS
Bright red, claw-shaped, tubular flowers are produced in a single whorl, surrounded by red-green, leaflike bracts. They attract butterflies and, in North America, hummingbirds. Whole heads, or individual florets, can be dried for potpourri, retaining color and scent well.

STEM
Squarish, light green, and hairy. It is little-branched, and tends to be red-tinged where the leaves join it.

CARE
Cut down dead stems in autumn. Mulch with well-rotted manure or compost in spring.

SEEDS
Very large, narrowly oblong, and edible. They have a ridged, shiny surface, and are green at first, ripening to dark brown. They lack the aniseed flavor of the foliage.

FLOWERS
Tiny white flowers, produced in flat-topped clusters similar to those of cow parsley.

Myrrhis odorata
SWEET CICELY
UMBELLIFERAE

According to John Gerard, the Elizabethan herbalist, sweet cicely "is very good for old people that are dull and without courage." The anise-scented foliage has a sweetening effect, and reduces acidity in stewed fruit.

HABIT Large, hardy perennial with downy, anise-scented leaves.

HEIGHT 3–6 ft (1–2 m).

SPREAD 2–4 ft (60 cm–1.2 m).

REMARKS A graceful plant for humus-rich soil, enjoying sun or shade providing conditions are moist. Use it as a foil to showier herbs, such as bee balm (*Monarda didyma*), or in a woodland border with elder (*Sambucus nigra*).

CARE
Easily grown from seed; sow outdoors in autumn, since it needs a period of cold for germination. Cut down dead foliage in autumn. Mulch with leaf mold and well-rotted manure or compost in spring. Self-sows in most gardens.

LEAVES
Highly divided, fernlike, and light green. Often speckled white, with a soft texture.

STEM
Hollow, downy, and furrowed.

Myrtus communis
MYRTLE
MYRTACEAE

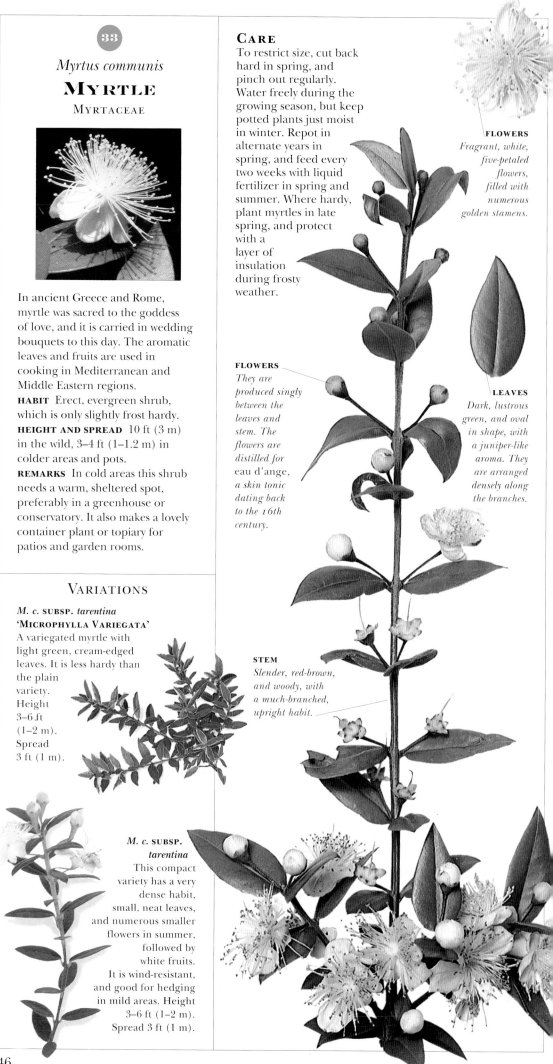

In ancient Greece and Rome, myrtle was sacred to the goddess of love, and it is carried in wedding bouquets to this day. The aromatic leaves and fruits are used in cooking in Mediterranean and Middle Eastern regions.

HABIT Erect, evergreen shrub, which is only slightly frost hardy.

HEIGHT AND SPREAD 10 ft (3 m) in the wild, 3–4 ft (1–1.2 m) in colder areas and pots.

REMARKS In cold areas this shrub needs a warm, sheltered spot, preferably in a greenhouse or conservatory. It also makes a lovely container plant or topiary for patios and garden rooms.

VARIATIONS

M. c. SUBSP. *tarentina*
'MICROPHYLLA VARIEGATA'
A variegated myrtle with light green, cream-edged leaves. It is less hardy than the plain variety. Height 3–6 ft (1–2 m). Spread 3 ft (1 m).

M. c. SUBSP.
tarentina
This compact variety has a very dense habit, small, neat leaves, and numerous smaller flowers in summer, followed by white fruits. It is wind-resistant, and good for hedging in mild areas. Height 3–6 ft (1–2 m). Spread 3 ft (1 m).

CARE
To restrict size, cut back hard in spring, and pinch out regularly. Water freely during the growing season, but keep potted plants just moist in winter. Repot in alternate years in spring, and feed every two weeks with liquid fertilizer in spring and summer. Where hardy, plant myrtles in late spring, and protect with a layer of insulation during frosty weather.

FLOWERS
Fragrant, white, five-petaled flowers, filled with numerous golden stamens.

FLOWERS
They are produced singly between the leaves and stem. The flowers are distilled for eau d'ange, a skin tonic dating back to the 16th century.

LEAVES
Dark, lustrous green, and oval in shape, with a juniper-like aroma. They are arranged densely along the branches.

STEM
Slender, red-brown, and woody, with a much-branched, upright habit.

STEM
Erect, branched, hairy, and square in cross-section, with the same pungent aroma as the leaves.

LEAVES
Gray-green, heart-shaped to oval, with a hairy surface, toothed margins, and a mint-thyme aroma. They dry well, and can be used for stuffing cat toys.

34

Nepeta cataria

CATNIP

LABIATAE

Catnip contains compounds that have a stimulant effect on cats, who chew the plant and roll in it.
HABIT Hardy perennial with an upright habit, and leaves with a pungent aroma. White, purple-spotted, tubular flowers are borne in summer and early autumn.
HEIGHT 1–3 ft (30 cm–1 m).
SPREAD 2 ft (60 cm).
REMARKS Not as attractive as the catmints, so best at the back of a border, or where damage by cats will not matter. Grow it among tidier, more colorful herbs, such as evening primroses (*Oenothera biennis*) and opium poppies (*Papaver somniferum*).

VARIATION

N. racemosa
(SYN. **N. mussinii**)
This bushy variety makes a good ornamental plant, but is less attractive to cats than *N. cataria*. Height and spread 18 in (45 cm).

SEEDS
Seed cases contain four smooth, oval, dark brown nutlets with a white mark at each end. They are viable for several years.

CARE
Cut back dead stems in autumn, and at any time plants look untidy. Mulch with well-rotted manure or compost in spring. Cover young plants with netting to protect them against cats until they are large enough to withstand attention. Stake mature plants in spring to minimize any damage.

47

Ocimum basilicum
BASIL
LABIATAE

This sweetly aromatic herb is
tropical Asian in origin, but has
become indispensable in Italian
cooking. It is traditionally grown
in Hindu homes and around
temples as a sacred plant.

HABIT Tender annual with
an upright, branched habit.

HEIGHT 8–24 in (20–60 cm).

SPREAD 6–12 in (15–30 cm).

REMARKS Basil is rarely successful
in the open ground in areas with
cool summers, but does well in pots.
Combine its lush foliage with curly
parsley, or plant several varieties
together. The small-leaved bush
basil and purple-leaved 'Dark Opal'
have distinctive, contrasting foliage.

SEEDS
*Seed cases contain
four brown, tear-
shaped nutlets.*

LEAVES
*Broadly oval and bright
green, barely toothed, and
up to 2 in (5 cm) long.
They are thin in texture,
and have an intense,
clovelike aroma.*

STEM
*Light green,
branched, round
at the base, and
becoming square
in cross-section
higher up.*

FLOWERS
*White, tubular,
two-lipped flowers,
0.3 in (8 mm)
long, are produced
in summer in
whorled spikes.*

CARE
Basil needs ample
warmth and light, so seed
should not be sown until
late spring, maintaining a
minimum temperature of
55°F (13°C). Pot individually,
or put three in a 10 in (25 cm)
pot when large enough to handle.
Pots of seedlings can also be
bought in supermarkets and
divided for growing in pots.
For a succession of young
leaves for cutting, sow in trays
at intervals of three weeks
throughout the summer.

O. b. VAR. 'CITRIODORUM' (LEMON BASIL)
A basil from northwest India, with a bushy habit, narrowly oval leaves, and white flowers. It has a refreshing citrus scent. Height 18–24 in (45–60 cm). Spread 10–14 in (25–35 cm).

O. b. VAR. *crispum* (CURLY BASIL)
A robust basil with large, extravagantly ruffled leaves, and a fine flavor. It is often called 'Neapolitana'. Height 8–24 in (20–60 cm). Spread 6–18 in (15–45 cm).

O. b. 'ANISE'
Originally from Persia, this variety has distinctive purple stems, purple-veined leaves, and light pink flowers. It has a sweet, anise-licorice aroma, and is sometimes called 'Licorice.' Height 18 in (45 cm). Spread 12 in (30 cm).

O. b. VAR. *minimum* (BUSH BASIL, GREEK BASIL)
This dwarf, compact variety is hardier than the species. It has very small leaves, less than 0.4 in (1 cm) long, and a reasonably good flavor. It makes a neat plant for pots. Height and spread 6–12 in (15–30 cm).

O. b. 'DARK OPAL' ('PURPUREUM')
An attractive variety with deep purple-black leaves and cerise pink flowers. Plant with mixed culinary, or gray-leaved, herbs. Height 2 ft (60 cm). Spread 12 in (30 cm).

O. b. 'PURPLE RUFFLES'
This variety is similar to 'Dark Opal,' but with ruffled, deeply toothed leaves. It makes a splendid specimen plant for containers. Height and spread 18–24 in (45–60 cm).

49

36

Oenothera biennis

EVENING PRIMROSE

ONAGRACEAE

Source of an oil that corrects hormonal imbalances, evening primroses are easily grown even in the poorest soils. They are related to fuchsias, not primroses.

HABIT Tall, erect biennial with large flowers opening at dusk in summer and early autumn.

HEIGHT 1–5 ft (30 cm–1.5 m).

SPREAD 9–12 in (23–30 cm).

REMARKS Plant near seats and entrances to enjoy the evening primrose's night-scented flowers. Sown early in spring, plants may flower the first year, and thereafter usually self-sow prolifically.

FLOWERS
Yellow, four-petaled flowers, up to 2 in (5 cm) across, open at twilight from pointed, red-flushed buds. They are pollinated by moths, which they attract with a sweet scent.

CARE
Thin out seedlings to 12 in (30 cm) apart. Remove dead flowers regularly to prevent excessive self-seeding.

LEAVES
Narrow, pointed leaves, often with red midribs, and up to 8 in (20 cm) long. They are arranged in a rosette at the base, becoming progressively shorter up the stem.

SEEDS
Capsules contain numerous light brown oval seeds, A single plant produces thousands of seeds, which in some gardens germinate in weedlike numbers.

STEM
Erect, stout, sometimes hairy, and usually simple, often with reddish speckles.

VARIATIONS

O. majorana (SWEET MARJORAM)
This half-hardy perennial has velvety, gray-green, oval leaves. Height 2 ft (60 cm). Spread 18 in (45 cm).

O. v. 'GOLD TIP'
A fine foliage plant in spring, with each leaf symmetrically tipped yellow. Height and spread 12–30 in (30–75 cm).

O. onites (POT MARJORAM)
A hardy, shrubby perennial with downy leaves. Height and spread 2 ft (60 cm).

O. v. 'AUREUM'
The most popular variety, with small, yellow-green leaves. Height and spread 30 in (75 cm).

Origanum vulgare

MARJORAM & OREGANO
LABIATAE

All marjorams have a long flowering period, and attract butterflies and bees. Plants grown in hot, dry areas have the strongest aroma.

HABIT Variable, hardy perennial with a bushy habit, and broadly oval, aromatic leaves.
HEIGHT 18 in (45 cm).
SPREAD 18 in (45 cm).
REMARKS Marjorams are subtle in color, shape, and texture, and harmonize well with other Mediterranean herbs that enjoy sunny, warm, and dry conditions. These include thymes (*Thymus* species) and savories (*Satureja*).

FLOWERS
Mauve to pink or white, bell-shaped, tubular flowers are borne in branched clusters.

LEAVES
Variable leaves, with a peppery, thymelike aroma. They may be hairy or smooth, oval to rounded, and pointed or blunt.

STEM
More or less upright, light purple-brown, and hairy. It roots at the base.

CARE
For the best flavor, grow oregano in the sunniest, warmest position possible. Cut back dead stems to ground level in winter. Trim after flowering to encourage a flush of new leaves.

38

Papaver rhoeas

CORN POPPY

PAPAVERACEAE

Poppies contain painkilling compounds, which are extracted from the green capsules. They are also cultivated for their seeds, which are used in baking and for an almond-flavored salad oil.

HABIT Hardy annual with a slender taproot and red blooms in summer.
HEIGHT 8–24 in (20–60 cm).
SPREAD 6–12 in (15–30 cm).
REMARKS Useful for filling gaps, or for a special area of annual herbs. To collect seed or to dry capsules for ornamental use, cut the stems before they start to turn brown, and hang upside down over a sheet of paper. The capsules will shed seeds as the "pepperpot" opens.

SEEDS
Numerous, tiny, dark brown seeds are contained in a flat-topped, tulip-shaped to rounded capsule, 0.4–0.8 in (1–2 cm) long.

FLOWERS
Bright red, four-petaled flowers, usually with a dark spot at the base of each petal, open from oval, bristly buds. They are short-lived, lasting less than a day.

CARE
Poppies do not transplant successfully. Sow seed where the plants are to flower, thinning to 12 in (30 cm) apart. To prevent excessive self-seeding, remove seed capsules as they form.

STEM
Light green, upright stems, which are clad in stiff hairs.

VARIATION

P. somniferum (OPIUM POPPY)
Hardy annual with waxy leaves. All parts are poisonous. It is illegal to grow opium poppies of any variety in some countries. Height 26 in–3 ft (65 cm–1 m). Spread 9 in–3 ft (23 cm–1 m).

LEAVES
Bright green, deeply cut and lobed, and roughly oval to narrowly oval in outline, with bristly hairs on the undersurface.

VARIATIONS

P. 'PRINCE OF ORANGE'
An orange-scented hybrid
with a compact habit, and
green, fan-shaped leaves.
Height and spread
2 ft (60 cm).

P. citronellum
Upright and bushy shrub,
with deeply veined leaves.
Height 1–3 ft (30cm–1 m).
Spread 1–2 ft (30–60 cm).

P. odoratissimum
(APPLE GERANIUM)
Low-growing shrub, with
light green, rounded leaves.
Height 12 in (30 cm).
Spread 2 ft (60 cm).

P. quercifolium
(OAK-LEAVED GERANIUM)
This upright shrub has
rough, sticky leaves.
Height 18–24 in (45–60 cm).
Spread 3 ft (1 m).

39

Pelargonium capitatum
ROSE-SCENTED GERANIUM
GERANIACEAE

Southern African in origin, scented
geraniums have demure colors,
a wide range of aromas, and
appealing leaf shapes and textures.
HABIT Tender, shrubby, evergreen
perennial with sage green, crinkled
leaves, which are rose-scented.
HEIGHT 1–2 ft (30–60 cm).
SPREAD 12–18 in (30–45 cm).
REMARKS Grow in pots beside
seats and entrances, where you
can enjoy their scent. They can also
be used as bedding plants, to fill
gaps in the herb garden, and in
mild areas may survive outdoors
in very sunny, sheltered spots.

CARE
Cut back in early spring to
remove straggly growths,
and pinch out regularly
to encourage a bushy habit.
Plants grown in the open may
be lifted and brought under
cover for the winter; they
can be cut back hard
when potting.

STEM
*Hairy, green,
and quite brittle,
becoming woody
at the base.*

FLOWERS
*Mauve-pink, with purple
veining, in clusters of one
to twenty. They are about
0.8 in (2 cm) across,
which is relatively large for
a scented geranium.*

LEAVES
*Soft, green,
velvety, and crinkled,
with irregularly lobed
margins. They have a
rose scent, and are the
source of geranium oil .*

Petroselinum crispum

PARSLEY

UMBELLIFERAE

Although often discarded as a garnish, parsley is one of the most beneficial herbs to include in the diet. Its leaves are rich in vitamins A and C, minerals, and compounds that clear toxins from the system.

HABIT Hardy biennial, usually grown as an annual, with triangular leaves. Tiny yellow-green flowers are produced in flat-topped clusters in the summer of the second year.

HEIGHT 15 in (38 cm), reaching 32 in (80 cm) when flowering.

SPREAD 12 in (30 cm).

REMARKS One of the most ornamental culinary herbs. Plant it as a contrast to plain-leaved herbs such as sorrel (*Rumex acetosa*).

SEEDS
Curved, oval, gray-brown, and 0.1 in (3 mm) long. They have a ridged surface and are aromatic, with a strong parsley flavor.

LEAVES
Rich green, aromatic, and triangular in outline. Divided into diamond-shaped, toothed leaflets, which in cultivated plants have densely curled margins.

STEM
Light green, solid, and succulent, with a ribbed surface and a strong aroma.

VARIATION

P. c. 'ITALIAN'
(PLAIN-LEAVED PARSLEY)
This has dark green, flat foliage with a strong flavor. Plants have long stalks and are large and weather-resistant, making them better suited to the open ground than to containers. Height and spread 15–24 in (38–60 cm).

ROOT
Thick, white-fleshed taproot with a stronger parsley flavor than stems or leaves.

CARE
Sow seed at intervals from late winter to early summer for a year-round supply. Seeds are slow to germinate, taking three to six weeks, unless soaked overnight in warm water before sowing. In cold areas, over–wintering plants need a sunny, sheltered position.

VARIATIONS

R. rugosa (RUGOSA ROSE)
A very hardy, deciduous shrub with dense, prickly stems, dark green leaves that turn yellow in autumn, and scented, single, purple-pink (or pink or white) flowers in summer. Makes an excellent hedge.

R. gallica 'VERSICOLOR' (ROSA MUNDI)
This variety has a similar habit to the Apothecary's rose, and bears semidouble, slightly scented flowers, which are pale pink with deep pink stripes. Height 30 in (75 cm). Spread 3 ft (1 m).

R. g. VAR. officinalis (APOTHECARY'S ROSE)
A neat, bushy, deciduous shrub, with bristly stems and leathery leaves. The flowers are pink.

Rosa canina
DOG ROSE
ROSACEAE

Roses have long been important in skin products, perfumery, medicine, and food flavoring. The dog rose is the heraldic emblem of England, and the origin of the "English rose" complexion.

HABIT Hardy, deciduous shrub with pink to white, scented flowers in summer, followed by scarlet hips.

HEIGHT 10 ft (3 m).

SPREAD 10 ft (3 m).

REMARKS Rather rampant for general garden use, but if space allows, plant in shrub collections or naturalize. Train on a frame to control arching stems. It can also be incorporated into large, informal hedges.

FLOWERS
Pink to white, fragrant, five-petaled flowers produced in clusters of up to four in summer. They are single and short-lived.

LEAVES
Midgreen, smooth, and mostly divided into five or seven oval, toothed leaflets.

CARE
Remove dead or damaged stems, and weak growths in early winter. Dog roses flower on the previous year's growth, and should not be cut back hard.

PETALS
These keep their scent when dried and can be used for potpourris.

FRUITS
Bright red, shiny, egg-shaped hips, which ripen in autumn.

STEM
Vigorous, arching, and green, climbing by means of stout, downward curving thorns.

Rosmarinus officinalis

ROSEMARY

LABIATAE

Rosemary symbolizes friendship, loyalty, and remembrance. Its name means "dew of the sea" – it grows wild on the coast, and the pale blue flowers can look like dew.

HABIT Variable, evergreen shrub, with an upright to spreading habit. It is slightly frost hardy, but plants vary in hardiness according to origin, age, and conditions.

HEIGHT 6 ft (2 m).

SPREAD 5–6 ft (1.5–2 m).

REMARKS This decorative shrub makes an excellent container plant, and also thrives in dry conditions on steep banks and gravel drives. It is a good contrast to larger-leaved, evergreen herbs.

LEAVES
Leathery, tough, and needlelike, with blunt ends. They have a dark green upper surface, pale downy underside, and a strong, resinous scent.

SEEDS
Seed cases contain four small, smooth, light brown nutlets.

STEM
Upright to spreading, brown, woody branches, with mostly four-angled stems. Branches are brittle, breaking easily under pressure.

FLOWERS
Borne in small clusters in spring in the leaf axils. Individual flowers are ice blue, tubular, and two-lipped, with the lower lip much larger and three-lobed.

VARIATIONS

R. o. PROSTRATUS GROUP (CREEPING ROSEMARY)
An ideal rosemary for containers, walls, and banks, with a low, spreading habit. It is slightly hardy, needing a very sunny, sheltered position. Sometimes called *R. lavandulaceus.* Height 6–12 in (15–30 cm). Spread 2–3 ft (60 cm–1 m).

R. o. 'FOTA BLUE'
Variable and rather tender, this rosemary is semi-prostrate, with dark blue flowers. Height 12–18 in (30–45 cm). Spread 2–3 ft (60 cm–1 m).

R. o. 'AUREUS' (GILDED ROSEMARY)
An unusual variety with irregular yellow variegation. It is not conspicuous from a distance, but gives added interest to potted plants. Plant it with gold-variegated bay, marjoram, or sage. Height 6 ft (2 m). Spread 5–6 ft (1.5–2 m).

R. o. VAR. *albiflorus*
The white-flowered rosemary is an excellent plant for white borders and for floral tributes. Height 6 ft (2 m). Spread 5–6 ft (1.5–2 m).

R. o. 'MAJORCA PINK'
A tender variety with an arching habit, small, dull green leaves, and mauve-pink flowers. Height 4 ft (1.2 m). Spread 1–2 ft (30–60 cm).

CARE
Remove dead stems and weak shoots in spring. Trim again after flowering to control shape. Rosemary dislikes cold, wet winters. Plants may rot at the roots, remaining green above ground until late spring. They rarely recover, but cuttings may be rooted successfully before the plant dies. Protect in severe weather, or bring indoors where not hardy.

R. o. 'MISS JESSOPP'S UPRIGHT'
A good plant for the formal herb garden and confined spaces, since it has a vigorous, upright habit. It is one of the hardier varieties. Height 6 ft (2 m). Spread 5–6 ft (1.5–2 m).

R. o. 'BENENDEN BLUE'
This small-growing variety has narrow, green foliage and a dense, cascading habit. It is very good for containers. Height and spread 2 ft (60 cm).

Rumex acetosa
SORREL
POLYGONACEAE

Popular since at least Roman times as a pot herb, sorrel comes somewhere between a herb and a vegetable. Though too astringent to eat in the same quantities as spinach, its acidic flavor is pleasant in salads and soups.
HABIT Hardy perennial with docklike leaves and tall spikes of reddish green flowers in summer.
HEIGHT 20–36 in (50 cm–1 m).
SPREAD 10–18 in (25–45 cm).
REMARKS Sorrel's simple, broad leaves provide a contrast to the foliage of curly parsley (*Petroselinum crispum*) and wild strawberry (*Fragaria vesca*). The leaves become more astringent as they age.

VARIATIONS

R. scutatus
(FRENCH SORREL, BUCKLER-LEAF SORREL)
Hardy, low-growing perennial, woody at the base, with long-stalked, shield-shaped leaves. It is less acidic than *R. acetosa*.

R. scutatus
'SILVER SHIELD'
The most ornamental sorrel, with silver-green leaves and green flowers. It is good as groundcover and for softening the edges of borders. Height 6–18 in (15–45 cm). Spread 4 ft (1.2 m).

LEAVES
Broad, oblong, and bright green, with a long stalk and arrow-shaped base. Lower leaves are up to 6 in (15 cm) long, becoming smaller, with shorter stalks higher up the stem.

SEEDS
Small, brown, shiny, pointed, and three-sided.

STEM
Red-tinged and juicy, with a ridged surface.

CARE
For a long period of leaf production, remove flower spikes as they appear. For winter supply, cover plants with cloches or keep pots of sorrel frost-free under glass.

SEEDS
Capsules with four or five lobes split open when ripe, shedding tiny black seeds.

FLOWERS
Mustard yellow flowers, with four fringed petals, are borne in open clusters in summer.

LEAVES
Blue-green and deeply divided, with club-shaped lobes and an aroma resembling wet paint.

44

Ruta graveolens
RUE
RUTACEAE

Rue was once renowned as an antidote to poisons and infectious diseases. It also had a reputation for improving eyesight and was used by Renaissance artists.
HABIT Hardy, evergreen subshrub with pungently aromatic leaves.
HEIGHT 2 ft (60 cm).
SPREAD 18 in (45 cm).
REMARKS One of the best shrubs for confined spaces, with a dense, compact habit and neat foliage that remains in good condition all year. For winter effect, plant next to purple sage (*Salvia officinalis* 'Purpurascens'); and in summer, try it beside pink bee balm (*Monarda* 'Croftway Pink').

VARIATIONS

***R. g.* 'JACKMAN'S BLUE'**
An outstanding foliage plant, with steely blue leaves. Height 2 ft (60 cm). Spread 18 in (45 cm).

***R. g.* 'VARIEGATA'**
This variety has irregular cream variegation, and the occasional entirely white leaf. Height 2 ft (60 cm). Spread 18 in (45 cm).

CARE
Prune hard in spring to maintain compact shape, but do not cut into main stem. Wear gloves since it contains compounds that can cause severe skin irritation.

STEM
Blue-green and becoming woody at the base.

45

Salvia officinalis
SAGE
LABIATAE

Sage has long been revered as a longevity herb. It is also one of the most widely used culinary herbs, and an excellent garden plant.
HABIT Hardy, evergreen shrub with aromatic leaves and spikes of purple-blue, two-lipped flowers.
HEIGHT 24–32 in (60–80 cm).
SPREAD 3 ft (1 m).
REMARKS The soft color and texture of sage is a perfect foil for the spiky leaves of rosemary (*Rosmarinus officinalis*) and thyme (*Thymus* species). Its simple foliage is also effective with the finely cut leaves of artemisias (*Artemisia* species), and makes a good contrast to dark, glossy evergreens.

VARIATIONS

S.o. 'PURPURASCENS' (PURPLE SAGE)
This sage has purple-gray, velvety leaves. Height 24–32 in (60–80 cm). Spread 3 ft (1 m).

S.o. 'KEW GOLD'
A pretty sage with yellow foliage and a compact habit. It is especially effective with yellow- and orange-flowered herbs. Height 12 in (30 cm). Spread 18 in (45 cm).

S. sclarea (CLARY SAGE)
A fast-growing, tall biennial with aromatic, oval leaves, and spikes of flowers. Height 3 ft (1 m). Spread 2 ft (60 cm).

S.o. 'ICTERINA'
The yellow-variegated leaves of this variety can be used to add interest to the plain greens of parsley, bay, and chives. Height 24–32 in (60–80 cm). Spread 3 ft (1 m).

LEAVES
Oval, pointed, and pale gray-green, with a velvety surface.

STEM
Much-branched, four-angled, and finely downy, becoming woody at the base.

CARE
Sage bushes tend to become woody and sparse with age, so plan to replace plants after their fourth or fifth year. They are easily propagated from cuttings. Variants will not come true from seed.

VARIATION

S. n. 'GUINCHO PURPLE' (PURPLE ELDER)
This variety has dark purple-bronze foliage and pink-stamened, cream flowers. Height and spread 20 ft (6 m).

STEM
Arching stems have corky, gray-brown bark. They are brittle, and when broken have the same fetid smell as the leaves.

CARE
Elder comes into leaf very early in the year, so prune hard in late winter before the buds swell. If grown for its foliage, rather than for flowers and fruits, cut back to within 12 in (30 cm) of ground level, which will encourage strong new shoots from the base.

Sambucus nigra
ELDER
CAPRIFOLIACEAE

Elder has provided remedies for most common complaints, from colds and flu to skin problems. Elderflower water remains popular in cosmetics, and both flowers and berries make country wines.
HABIT Hardy, deciduous, shrubby tree with attractive flowers.
HEIGHT 15–30 ft (4.5–10 m).
SPREAD 12–15 ft (4–4.5 m).
REMARKS Though the varieties are more ornamental as garden shrubs, common elder is a good subject for informal hedges and wildflower gardens. Plant it as a background for other woodland herbs, such as sweet cicely (*Myrrhis odorata*) and foxgloves (*Digitalis purpurea*).

FLOWERS
Cream flowers, 0.2 in (5 mm) across, are produced in flat-topped clusters, 4–8 in (10–20 cm) across, in early summer. Their scent has been compared to muscatel wine.

LEAVES
Divided into five to seven oval leaflets, and tapering toward the tip. Elder leaves may turn bronze, cream, and pink in autumn.

47

Santolina chamaecyparissus
LAVENDER
COTTON
COMPOSITAE

Grown by the ancient Greeks and Romans, lavender cotton became popular in northern Europe during the 16th century as a knot-garden plant. Its foliage repels insects.

HABIT Hardy, aromatic, evergreen shrub with narrow gray leaves.

HEIGHT 8–20 in (20–50 cm).

SPREAD 2 ft (60 cm).

REMARKS The neat, silver-gray foliage of lavender cotton makes an excellent dwarf hedge. In a knot-garden it provides contrast to dark green hedging plants, such as boxwood (*Buxus sempervirens* 'Suffruticosa').

FLOWERS
Solitary heads of tightly packed, tubular florets, deep yellow in color, are produced on slender gray stalks. They are long-lasting.

LEAVES
Narrow, silver-gray, and woolly. They are finely divided into closely packed, blunt segments, and have a pungent aroma.

CARE
To make a hedge, set young plants 12–15 in (30–38 cm) apart in spring, and pinch out growing points to encourage a bushy habit. Prune twice a year, in spring and again after flowering. Trim lightly to shape several times during the growing season.

STEM
Gray-green and woolly, becoming brown and woody at the base.

VARIATIONS

S. c. 'LEMON QUEEN'
This variety has cream flowers. Height 10–16 in (25–40 cm). Spread 12–20 in (30–50 cm).

S. pinnata SUBSP. neapolitana
A rounded shrub with gray-green woolly leaves. Height 30 in (75 cm). Spread 3 ft (1 m).

S. rosmarinifolia (SYN. S. virens) (HOLYFLAX)
Unlike most lavender cottons, this kind has bright green leaves. Yellow flowers appear in summer. Height 2 ft (60 cm). Spread 3 ft (1 m).

VARIATION

S. o. 'DAZZLER'
A variety with cream-splashed foliage. Shoots that revert to plain green should be removed as they appear.
Height 2 ft (60 cm).
Spread 12 in (30 cm).

FLOWERS
Clusters of scented flowers, about 1 in (2.5 cm) across, resembling small pinks.

Saponaria officinalis
SOAPWORT
CARYOPHYLLACEAE

Before commercial soap production began in the 1800s, soapwort was grown in cottage gardens to make soap suds for washing. It is long-lived, often found in derelict gardens, and late-flowering – hence the name "goodbye-to-summer."

HABIT Hardy perennial with creeping rhizomes and broadly oval, pointed leaves.

HEIGHT 1–3 ft (30 cm–1 m).

SPREAD 2 ft (60 cm).

REMARKS A vigorous perennial for the border. Its flowers look pretty against dark plants, such as purple elder (*Sambucus nigra* 'Guincho Purple'), or with the mauve spikes of flowering mints.

CARE
Stake in early summer to prevent flopping as flower heads develop. Tends to be invasive, so divide each year, or plant near other large, vigorous herbs. Cut back dead stems in winter. Do not plant where roots or foliage may contact pond water, since soapwort is poisonous to fish.

FLOWERS
Usually pale pink and single in the wild, but double-flowered and rose pink varieties are common in gardens.

STEM
Sturdy, more or less upright, and green, often maroon-tinged towards the base. It contains lather-producing soaplike compounds known as saponins.

LEAVES
Broadly oval and pointed, with three distinct, parallel main veins.

Satureja montana
WINTER SAVORY
LABIATAE

Winter savory has a stronger flavor than summer savory, and can be picked fresh from the garden all year round, even in winter. Savory is known as "the bean herb," since its peppery, thymelike aroma has an affinity with legumes of all kinds.

HABIT Hardy, shrubby perennial with small, narrow, evergreen leaves, which are strongly aromatic.
HEIGHT 15 in (38 cm).
SPREAD 8 in (20 cm).
REMARKS Winter savory is a typical Mediterranean herb, thriving on sun-baked, stony hillsides. Grow it with thyme (*Thymus* species) or marjoram (*Origanum* species), or plant as a dwarf, informal hedge.

VARIATIONS

S. spicigera
(SYN. *S. repandra*)
(CREEPING SAVORY)
Hardy, prostrate shrublet with narrow, aromatic leaves and white flowers in summer. It needs no pruning.
Height 2.4 in (6 cm).
Spread 12 in (30 cm).

S. hortensis
(SUMMER SAVORY)
Hardy annual with one wide-branching stem, and short-stalked, aromatic leaves.
Height 4–15 in (10–38cm).
Spread 7–30 in (17–75 cm).

LEAVES
Stalkless, narrow, pointed, and up to 1.1 in (3 cm) long. They are strongly aromatic, with a spicy, thymelike aroma.

FLOWERS
Small, white to pale pink or purple flowers in whorls of up to fourteen. The petals are fused into a two-lipped tube, typical of the Labiatae *family.*

STEM
Smooth to minutely hairy stems, becoming woody at the base.

CARE
For hedges, plant 9 in (23 cm) apart, and pinch out to encourage bushy growth. Prune established plants in spring and autumn. Fertilize lightly, since excessive feeding produces weak growth.

VARIATION

S. t. 'ROYAL RUBY'
One of several
varieties with a
pronounced deep
maroon flush,
especially toward
the center of
the rosette. Grow
it as a contrast to
the green varieties.
It does not come
true from seed.

Sempervivum tectorum

HEN-AND-CHICKENS
CRASSULACEAE

CARE
Hen-and-chickens are very
drought-resistant, and
rarely needing watering
when grown outdoors.
Propagation is easy,
by detaching plantlets
from the parent and
potting separately.

LEAVES
*The leaves contain a
mucilage with similar,
but weaker, healing
properties to* Aloe vera.

Grown in ornamental containers
during Roman times, and
traditionally planted on roofs as a
protection against lightning, hen-
and-chickens are one of the earliest
recorded "houseplants."

HABIT Hardy, evergreen, succulent
perennial. Each rosette of fleshy
leaves produces several smaller
rosettes before flowering and
dying, forming a large clump.

HEIGHT 2–3 in (5–8 cm).

SPREAD 12 in (30 cm).

REMARKS A trouble-free herb
that remains neat and attractive
all year round. Plant in pots or in
the crevices of walls and paving
slabs, and at the edges of paths.

LEAVES
*Thick, fleshy,
pointed, spine-
tipped leaves,
arranged in a
rosette. They are
predominantly green in
color with maroon tips,
flushing red after
prolonged drought.*

STEM
*A fleshy
runner
is produced by
the parent plant,
at the end of which
a plantlet develops.*

51

Symphytum officinale
COMFREY
BORAGINACEAE

This remarkable healing herb was once known as knitbone, because the leaves and roots were traditionally used in poultices to mend fractures.

HABIT Stout, hardy perennial with bristly, oval, tapering leaves. Purple to white, funnel-shaped flowers in a branched, coiled cluster in summer.

HEIGHT 2–4 ft (60 cm–1.2 m).

SPREAD 1–2 ft (30–60 cm).

REMARKS A vigorous plant, suitable for moist soil in a large herb garden, or a wildflower border. Plant with other large perennials, such as tansy (*Tanacetum vulgare*), soapwort (*Saponaria officinalis*), or sweet cicely (*Myrrhis odorata*).

STEM
Upright and much-branched, with bristly hairs.

VARIATIONS

S. asperum (PRICKLY COMFREY)
A stout, bristly plant with oval, pointed leaves. Height 4–6 ft (1.2–2 m). Spread 3–4 ft (1–1.2 m).

S. x uplandicum 'VARIEGATUM' (VARIEGATED RUSSIAN COMFREY)
This hybrid is best grown in semishade to avoid scorching of variegated areas. Height 3 ft (1 m). Spread 2 ft (60 cm).

FLOWERS
Drooping, bell-shaped flowers open in succession from coiled clusters of buds.

CARE
Consider the planting position carefully, since comfrey is deep-rooted and difficult to move when established, and any pieces of root left behind will regenerate. Cut down dead stems in winter. Comfrey is a rich feeder, so mulch with ample well-rotted manure or compost in the spring.

FLOWERS
Flowers are typically purple to mauve, but plants with white flowers are found occasionally.

LEAVES
Oval, tapering to the tip, and reaching 10 in (25 cm) long. Lower leaves have long stalks, and become stalkless higher up the stem. They have a thick midrib and a rough, bristly haired surface.

LEAVES
Pungently aromatic, deeply divided and sharply toothed, reaching 3 in (8 cm) long.

Tagetes patula
FRENCH MARIGOLD
COMPOSITAE

Mexican in origin, these familiar summer annuals are culinary and medicinal plants in their native country, and have been associated with religious festivals since pre-Columbian times.

HABIT Bushy, half-hardy annual with strongly aromatic leaves.

HEIGHT 12 in (30 cm).

SPREAD 12 in (30 cm).

REMARKS The bright colors and neat habit of these plants makes them ideal for summer bedding, edging, and containers. Plant them with contrasting purple basil (*Ocimum basilicum* 'Dark Opal').

CARE
Sow seed in spring at 64°F (18°C). Give seedlings separate pots when large enough to handle, and plant out as the first flowers show color, spacing 9–12 in (23–30 cm) apart. Deadhead regularly to prolong flowering.

SEEDS
Dark brown, rod-shaped and shiny, with a tuft of cream bristles.

FLOWERS
Variably colored, from yellow to orange and shades of red-brown, with wedge-shaped petals. They have the same pungent smell as the foliage.

STEM
Aromatic, erect, and green, shading to maroon and hollow at the base.

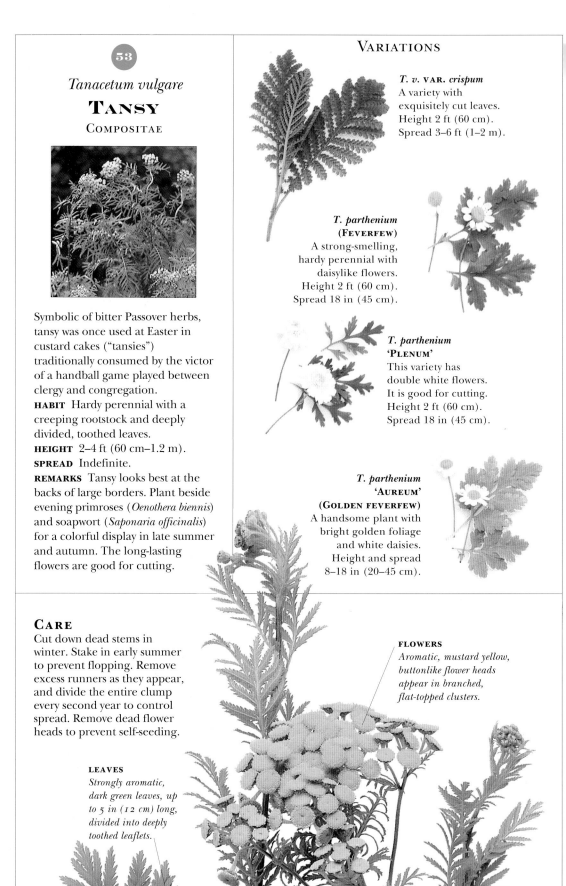

53

Tanacetum vulgare

TANSY

COMPOSITAE

Symbolic of bitter Passover herbs, tansy was once used at Easter in custard cakes ("tansies") traditionally consumed by the victor of a handball game played between clergy and congregation.

HABIT Hardy perennial with a creeping rootstock and deeply divided, toothed leaves.

HEIGHT 2–4 ft (60 cm–1.2 m).

SPREAD Indefinite.

REMARKS Tansy looks best at the backs of large borders. Plant beside evening primroses (*Oenothera biennis*) and soapwort (*Saponaria officinalis*) for a colorful display in late summer and autumn. The long-lasting flowers are good for cutting.

VARIATIONS

T. v. VAR. crispum
A variety with exquisitely cut leaves. Height 2 ft (60 cm). Spread 3–6 ft (1–2 m).

T. parthenium (FEVERFEW)
A strong-smelling, hardy perennial with daisylike flowers. Height 2 ft (60 cm). Spread 18 in (45 cm).

T. parthenium 'PLENUM'
This variety has double white flowers. It is good for cutting. Height 2 ft (60 cm). Spread 18 in (45 cm).

T. parthenium 'AUREUM' (GOLDEN FEVERFEW)
A handsome plant with bright golden foliage and white daisies. Height and spread 8–18 in (20–45 cm).

CARE

Cut down dead stems in winter. Stake in early summer to prevent flopping. Remove excess runners as they appear, and divide the entire clump every second year to control spread. Remove dead flower heads to prevent self-seeding.

FLOWERS
Aromatic, mustard yellow, buttonlike flower heads appear in branched, flat-topped clusters.

LEAVES
Strongly aromatic, dark green leaves, up to 5 in (12 cm) long, divided into deeply toothed leaflets.

CARE

Plant 6–9 in (15–23 cm) apart to form a continuous edging. Cut back in spring to maintain a compact habit. Remove dead flower spikes to encourage bushy new growth.

STEM
Upright to spreading, slender, dark green, and quite brittle.

Teucrium chamaedrys

WALL GERMANDER

LABIATAE

This Mediterranean herb has been used medicinally since ancient times, and was once famed as a cure for gout. It is now considered toxic, but remains very popular as a garden plant.

HABIT Hardy, shrubby perennial with a creeping rootstock.
HEIGHT 4–10 in (10–25 cm).
SPREAD 4–10 in (10–25 cm).
REMARKS A neat, modestly spreading plant for containers and for the edges of paths and beds. It is often confused in nurseries with the hedge germanders ·*T. divaricatum* and *T.* x *lucidrys*.

FLOWERS
Small, purple-pink, and two-lipped, in whorls of four to eight, appearing in summer and autumn.

LEAVES
Oval, often shiny, and neatly lobed, reaching 0.75 in (2 cm) long, and aromatic when crushed. They resemble miniature oak leaves hence the name chamaedrys, *meaning "ground oak."*

55

Thymus vulgaris
COMMON THYME
LABIATAE

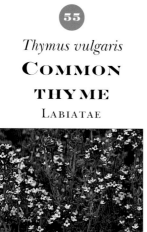

Though one of the smallest culinary herbs, thyme has no rival for fragrance. The tiny flowers produce large amounts of nectar, making thyme important also as a bee plant.
HABIT Variable, hardy shrub with pale mauve to white flowers.
HEIGHT 8–12 in (20–30 cm).
SPREAD 8–12 in (20–30 cm).
REMARKS Small and compact, thyme is indispensable for containers, and as an edging to paths and borders. Grow several different thymes together, varying in habit and color, and include common thyme for height.

VARIATIONS

T. serpyllum 'COCCINEUS' (RED-FLOWERED THYME)
A variety with bright magenta flowers. Height 0.4–3 in (1–7 cm). Spread 8 in (20 cm).

T. v. 'SILVER POSIE' (SILVER THYME)
This pretty variety has white-variegated leaves. Height and spread 10 in (25 cm).

T. pulegioides (BROAD-LEAVED THYME)
A sprawling shrub with a strong fragrance. Height 8 in (20 cm). Spread 16 in (40 cm).

T. × *citriodorus* (LEMON THYME)
An upright shrub with lemon-scented leaves. Height 9–12 in (23–30 cm). Spread 12–16 in (30–40 cm).

T. herba-barona (CARAWAY THYME)
A wiry, carpeting thyme with a caraway nutmeg aroma. Height 0.4–2 in (1–5 cm). Spread 10 in (25 cm).

CARE
Thyme dislikes hard pruning and wet winters. Trim lightly after flowering to remove dead flower heads and encourage compact growth. Protect thymes from mud-splashing and moisture in winter by a layer of grit. Keep plants free of fallen leaves in autumn.

LEAVES
Narrow, gray-green and downy, reaching only 0.3 in (8 mm) in length.

STEM
Pale brownish-green, four-angled, becoming woody in older plants.

FLOWERS
Delicate, five-petaled,
yellow flowers, up to
1.2 in (3 cm) across,
produced in stout spikes
in the second summer.

CARE
Remove all but one or two
dead flower spikes to prevent
excessive self-sowing. Weed
out seedlings, leaving only
the best-placed. Watch out
for caterpillars of mullein
moths, which seriously
damage foliage.

FLOWER BUDS
They open in
succession from
woolly buds from
midsummer to
mid-autumn.

Verbascum thapsus
MULLEIN
SCROPHULARIACEAE

Mullein featured in the epic travels
of Ulysses, protecting him from
the enchantress Circe. It has been
used medicinally since ancient
times to treat bronchial complaints.
HABIT Tall, hardy biennial with
large, woolly leaves. It has a long,
dense spike of flowers in summer.
HEIGHT 6 ft (2 m).
SPREAD 3 ft (1 m).
REMARKS A stately plant, providing
architectural interest in borders,
dry banks, and gravel areas. Use
it to punctuate silvery mounds
of artemisias (*Artemisia* species),
buckler-leaved sorrel (*Rumex*
scutatus), or lavender cotton
(*Santolina chamaecyparissus*).

SEEDS
Numerous tiny
brown seeds in each
capsule, which
measures 0.2–0.4 in
(7–10 mm) in length.

LEAVES
Gray-green, oval-oblong
in shape, with a soft,
woolly texture. Lower
leaves reach up to 18 in
(45 cm) long, and form
a rosette in the first year.

STEM
Thick, usually
unbranched, and
white-woolly. Dead stems
make excellent kindling.

57

Viburnum opulus
GUELDER ROSE
CAPRIFOLIACEAE

Guelder rose comes from the Dutch province of Gelderland, which was once a center for wild and cultivated varieties of this shrub. It is also known as cramp bark.

HABIT Hardy, deciduous shrub with flat-topped clusters of white flowers in summer, followed by poisonous, scarlet berries.

HEIGHT 12 ft (4 m).

SPREAD 12 ft (4 m).

REMARKS An excellent garden shrub with delightful flowers and early-ripening, brightly colored berries. Grow in rich, moist soil with other large herbs, such as elder (*Sambucus nigra*) and sweet cicely (*Myrrhis odorata*).

LEAVES
Dark green, up to 3 in (8 cm) in length, with three to five lobes, and irregularly toothed.

CARE

Plant out of reach of children. Remove any dead wood in spring, and thin out older shoots after flowering. Mulch with well-rotted manure or compost in spring.

FRUITS
Oval to round and glossy, ripening early to scarlet, in long-stalked clusters.

STEM
Branches are more or less erect, with smooth twigs and gray bark.

72

VARIATIONS

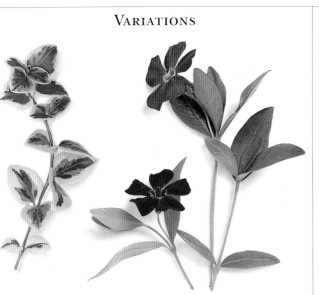

V. major
'VARIEGATA'
The most widely
grown variety,
with blue flowers.
Height 18 in
(45 cm). Spread
indefinite.

V. minor
'ATROPURPUREA'
An unusual form
with wine-red
flowers. Height
12 in (30 cm).
Spread
indefinite.

V. minor (LESSER PERIWINKLE)
This has narrow
leaves and small
flowers. Height
12 in (30 cm).
Spread
indefinite.

58

Vinca major
GREATER PERIWINKLE
APOCYNACEAE

Once known as "sorcerer's violet,"
periwinkle was thought to protect
against spirits and spells.
Its poisonous leaves contain
alkaloids, now used in drugs to
treat hardening of the arteries.
HABIT Hardy, evergreen subshrub
with glossy leaves and blue flowers.
HEIGHT 18 in (45 cm).
SPREAD Indefinite.
REMARKS One of the best
plants for groundcover in shade,
although it flowers more freely in
a sunny position. Plant beneath
trees and shrubs, or on exposed
banks to bind the soil.

LEAVES
Broadly oval, pointed,
and glossy, reaching
3 in (8 mm) in length,
on short stalks.

FLOWERS
Blue, propeller-
shaped, and about
1.6 in (4 cm) across,
appearing on short,
erect flowering stems.

STEM
Long, green, and slender,
with an arching or trailing
habit, rooting at the tips.

CARE
To control spread, remove
colonizing stems as they
appear, and cut back hard
in autumn or winter.

73

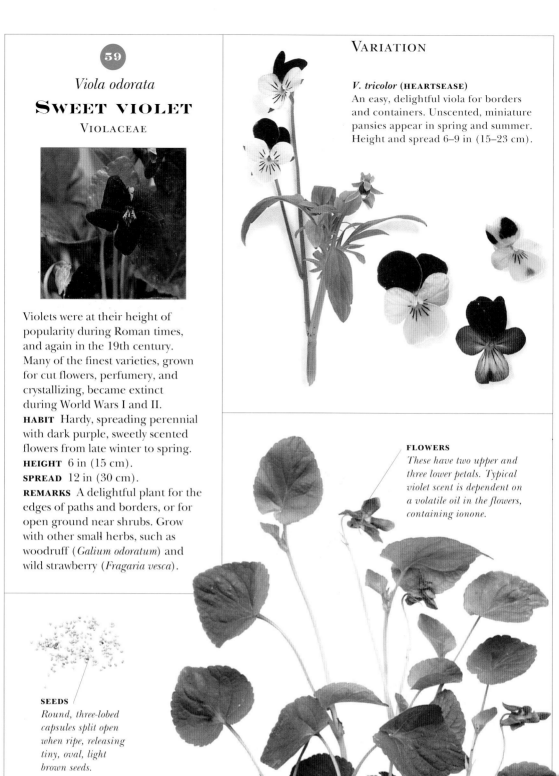

59

Viola odorata
SWEET VIOLET
VIOLACEAE

Violets were at their height of
popularity during Roman times,
and again in the 19th century.
Many of the finest varieties, grown
for cut flowers, perfumery, and
crystallizing, became extinct
during World Wars I and II.
HABIT Hardy, spreading perennial
with dark purple, sweetly scented
flowers from late winter to spring.
HEIGHT 6 in (15 cm).
SPREAD 12 in (30 cm).
REMARKS A delightful plant for the
edges of paths and borders, or for
open ground near shrubs. Grow
with other small herbs, such as
woodruff (*Galium odoratum*) and
wild strawberry (*Fragaria vesca*).

SEEDS
*Round, three-lobed
capsules split open
when ripe, releasing
tiny, oval, light
brown seeds.*

CARE
Mulch with well-rotted manure,
compost, or leaf mold in winter.
Sweet violets are easily propagated
by removing individual plantlets
that form on runners. Deadhead
to prolong flowering.

VARIATION

V. tricolor (HEARTSEASE)
An easy, delightful viola for borders
and containers. Unscented, miniature
pansies appear in spring and summer.
Height and spread 6–9 in (15–23 cm).

FLOWERS
*These have two upper and
three lower petals. Typical
violet scent is dependent on
a volatile oil in the flowers,
containing ionone.*

LEAVES
*Broadly oval to
heart-shaped, up
to 2.4 in (6 cm)
in length, with
long stalks and
indented margins.*

STEM
*Tough, brown
rhizomes and long,
creeping runners.*

VARIATION

V. agnus-castus
(**CHASTE TREE**)
This variety has clusters
of lilac flowers and leaves
divided into five to nine
slender leaflets. Height
and spread 15 ft (5 m).

CARE

Needs ample warmth
and sun to flower well,
so plant against a wall
in cold areas. It may
die back nearly to the
ground in a severe
winter, but usually
sprouts from the base.
In spring, cut back
last year's growths, and
feed with well-rotted
manure or compost.

60

Vitex negundo
CHINESE
CHASTE TREE
VERBENACEAE

The Chinese chaste tree has
been used in Chinese traditional
medicine for nearly 2,000 years.
Its Mediterranean relative,
V. agnus-castus, is used to treat
hormonal problems.
HABIT Frost-hardy, deciduous
shrub with aromatic leaves.
HEIGHT 15 ft (5 m).
SPREAD 15 ft (5 m).
REMARKS An elegant shrub and
an excellent bee plant. Grow in a
sunny border with other aromatic
shrubs, such as lemon verbena
(*Aloysia triphylla*) and balm of
Gilead (*Cedronella canariensis*).

FLOWERS
*Small, tubular,
lavender flowers
with a pleasant
scent and
copious nectar.*

FLOWER BUDS
*In Nepal, these
are used to treat
pneumonia.*

LEAVES
*Aromatic, divided into
three to five narrowly
oval, pointed leaflets,
with gray undersides.*

STEM
*Slender and woody, with
a smooth texture and
brownish green color.*

HARDINESS ZONES FOR VARIATIONS

A
Agastache rugosa
Zones 6–9

Alchemilla alpina
Zones 3–7

Allium schoenoprasum 'FORESCATE'
Zones 3–9

Allium tricoccum
Zones 4–7

Artemisia absinthium
'LAMBROOK SILVER'
Zones 5–9

Artemisia abrotanum
Zones 6–10

Artemisia annua
Frost-hardy annual

Artemisia arborescens
Zones 8–9

Artemisia caucasica (SYN. *A. lanata*)
Zones 4–7

Artemisia dracunculus
Zones 4–7

Artemisia lactiflora
Zones 5–8

Artemisia ludoviciana
'SILVER QUEEN'
Zones 5–9

B
Buxus sempervirens 'ELEGANTISSIMA'
Zones 5–8

Buxus sempervirens 'SUFFRUTICOSA'
Zones 5–8

C
Centaurea cyanus 'FLORENCE SERIES'
Hardy annual

Chamaemelum nobile 'FLORE PLENO'
Zones 3–8

Chamaemelum nobile 'TRENEAGUE'
Zones 3–8

D
Digitalis lanata
Zones 4–10

Digitalis lutea
Zones 4–10

E
Echinacea angustifolia
Zones 3–10

Eupatorium cannabinum
Zones 5–9

F
Foeniculum vulgare 'PURPUREUM'
Zones 4–10

Fragaria vesca 'VARIEGATA'
Zones 5–9

H
Helichrysum italicum SUBSP. *microphyllum*
Zones 8–9

Humulus lupulus 'AUREUS'
Zones 5–8

Hyssopus officinalis 'ALBUS'
Zones 3–9

Hyssopus officinalis 'NETHERFIELD'
Zones 3–9

Hyssopus officinalis FORMA *roseus*
Zones 3–9

L
Laurus nobilis 'ANGUSTIFOLIA'
Zones 8–10

Laurus nobilis 'AUREA'
Zones 8–10

Lavandula angustifolia 'HIDCOTE'
Zones 5–8

Lavandula angustifolia 'MUNSTEAD'
Zones 5–8

Lavandula angustifolia 'NANA ALBA'
Zones 5–8

Lavandula angustifolia SUBSP. *pedunculata*
Zones 8–9

Lavandula angustifolia 'ROSEA'
Zones 5–8

Lavandula dentata
Zones 5–9

Lavandula lanata
Zones 8–9

Lavandula 'SAWYER'S'
Zones 7–9

Lavandula stoechas
Zones 8–9

M
Matricaria recutita
Hardy annual

Melissa officinalis 'AUREA'
Zones 4–9

Mentha aquatica
Zones 6–11

Mentha x *gracilis* 'VARIEGATA'
Zones 7–9

Mentha spicata 'MOROCCAN'
Zones 4–9

Mentha suaveolens 'VARIEGATA'
Zones 7-9

Monarda didyma 'BLUE STOCKING'
Zones 4–9

Monarda didyma 'CROFTWAY PINK'
Zones 4–10

Monarda fistulosa
Zones 3–9

Myrtus communis SUBSP. *tarentina*
Zones 9–10

Myrtus communis SUBSP. *tarentina*
'MICROPHYLLA VARIEGATA'
Zones 10–11

N
Nepeta racemosa (SYN. *N. mussinnii*)
Zones 4–8

O
Ocimum basilicum
All variations are tender annuals

Origanum majorana
Zones 9–10

Origanum onites
Zones 8–10

Origanum vulgare 'AUREUM'
Zones 6–9

Origanum vulgare 'GOLD TIP'
Zones 8–9

P
Papaver somniferum
Hardy annual

Pelargonium
All variations are tender perennials

Petroselinum crispum 'ITALIAN'
Zones 6–9

R
Rosa gallica 'VERSICOLOR'
Zones 4–8

Rosa gallica VAR. *officinalis*
Zones 4–8

Rosa rugosa
Zones 2–8

Rosmarinus officinalis
All variations are zones 8–10

Rumex scutatus
Zones 4–8

Rumex scutatus 'SILVER SHIELD'
Zones 4–8

Ruta graveolens 'JACKMAN'S BLUE'
Zones 4–8

Ruta graveolens 'VARIEGATA'
Zones 4–8

S
Salvia officinalis 'ICTERINA'
Zones 7–9

Salvia officinalis 'KEW GOLD'
Zones 7–9

Salvia officinalis 'PURPURASCENS'
Zones 7–9

Salvia sclarea
Zones 4–9

Sambucus nigra 'GUINCHO PURPLE'
Zones 5–9

Santolina chamaecyparissus 'LEMON QUEEN'
Zones 6–8

Santolina pinnata SUBSP. *neapolitana*
Tender perennial

Santolina rosmarinifolia (SYN. *S. virens*)
Tender perennial

Saponaria officinalis 'DAZZLER'
Zones 2-8

Satureja hortensis
Hardy annual

Satureja spicigera (SYN. *S. repandra*)
Zones 7–8

Sempervivum tectorum 'ROYAL RUBY'
Zones 5–10

Symphytum asperum
Zone 5

Symphytum × uplandicum 'VARIEGATA'
Zones 4–9

T
Tanacetum parthenium
All variations are zones 4–9

Tanacetum vulgare VAR. *crispum*
Zones 4–9

Thymus × citriodorus
Zones 5–9

Thymus herba-barona
Zones 6–8

Thymus pulegioides
Zones 4–8

Thymus serpyllum 'COCCINEUS'
Zones 4–8

Thymus vulgaris 'SILVER POSIE'
Zones 7–8

V
Vinca major 'VARIEGATA'
Zones 7–9

Vinca minor
Zones 3–8

Vinca minor 'ATROPURPUREA'
Zones 3–8

Viola tricolor
Zones 4–9

Vitex agnus-castus
Zones 7–9

HARDINESS ZONE MAP

The map below shows the average lowest temperatures that can be expected each year in North America. These temperatures are based on the lowest temperatures recorded for the years 1974–86. The map shows 11 different zones: zones 1–10 represent progressively warmer areas of winter hardiness; zone 11 represents areas that have average annual minimum temperatures above 40°F (4°C) and are frost-free. Zone ratings indicate excellent adaptability of the plants. Many plants may survive in warmer or colder zones; mere survival, however, does not represent satisfactory performance.

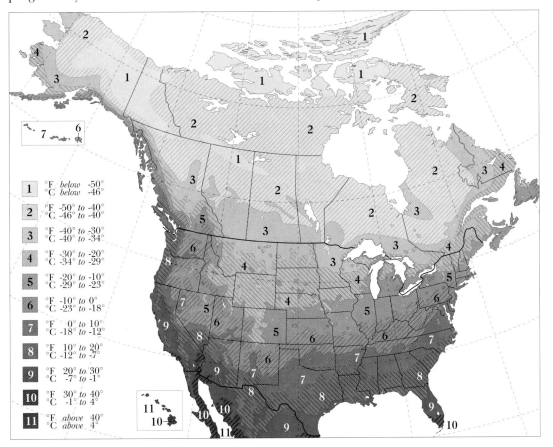

	°F	°C
1	below −50°	below −46°
2	−50° to −40°	−46° to −40°
3	−40° to −30°	−40° to −34°
4	−30° to −20°	−34° to −29°
5	−20° to −10°	−29° to −23°
6	−10° to 0°	−23° to −18°
7	0° to 10°	−18° to −12°
8	10° to 20°	−12° to −7°
9	20° to 30°	−7° to −1°
10	30° to 40°	−1° to 4°
11	above 40°	above 4°

INDEX

ACKNOWLEDGMENTS

PHOTOGRAPHY CREDITS

Key: t = top; tl = top left; tr = top right; tc = top center; cl = center left; cr = center right;
b = bottom; bl = bottom left; br = bottom right.

Photographs by Peter Anderson, Eric Crichton, Philip Dowell, Neil Fletcher, Steve Gorton,
Derek Hall, Stephen Hayward, Dave King, Andrew McKnobb, David Murray, and
Matthew Ward, except:

Deni Bown: 9br; 10cl; 11cr; 12tl; 14tl; 16tl; 17tr; 21tr and tl; 22tl; 23tr; 26tl; 27tr; 30tl; 31tr;
32tl; 34tl; 36tl; 38tl; 46cl and tl; 47tr; 48tl; 53tr and tc; 54tl; 55tr; 56tr; 58tl and tc; 59cr; 60tl;
61tl and tr; 63tl and tr; 65tl; 66tl; 69tr; 70tl and cr; 71tr; 72tl; 73tr and tl; 74tl; 75tr.
Bridgeman Art Library/British Library, London: 6b.
Geoff Dann: 24tl; 51tr.
E.T. Archive/Bodleian Library: 6t.
Royal Botanic Garden, Edinburgh: 20tl.
Neil Campbell Sharp: 8cl.
Clive Nichols: 2.
Harry Smith Collection: 10c; 39tr; 52tl.

Design assistance: Wendy Bartlet and Sarah Goodwin.

Editorial assistance: Annabel Morgan

Picture research: Lorna Ainger.

DK Picture Library: Ola Rudowska.